CW01237386

MILITARY OPERATIONS

of the

DUTCH ARMY

10th–17th May, 1940

P.L.G. Doorman, O.B.E.

Lieutenant-Colonel of the Dutch General Staff

Translated from the Dutch
by
S L Salzedo

Helion & Company Limited
26 Willow Road
Solihull
West Midlands
B91 1UE
England
Tel. 0121 705 3393
Fax 0121 711 4075
Email: publishing@helion.co.uk
Website: http://www.helion.co.uk

Published by Helion & Company Limited 2005
Originally published by the Netherlands Government Information Bureau, London, 1944 with the title *Military Operations in the Netherlands from 10th-17th May, 1940*

Designed and typeset by Helion & Company Ltd, Solihull, West Midlands
Cover designed by Bookcraft Limited, Stroud, Gloucestershire
Printed by The Cromwell Press, Trowbridge, Wiltshire

This edition © Helion & Company Limited 2004

ISBN 1 874622 72 8

British Library Cataloguing-in-Publication Data.
A catalogue record for this book is available from the British Library.

All rights reserved. No part of this publication may be reproduced, stored in a retrieval system, or transmitted, in any form, or by any means, electronic, mechanical, photocopying, recording or otherwise, without the express written consent of Helion & Company Limited.

Front cover illustration: Air defence machine gun in position, winter 1939/40. Rear cover illustrations: Evacuation of Dutch soldiers, Zeeland, May 1940. Both images appear courtesy of the Military History Section, Royal Netherlands Army

For details of other military history titles published by Helion & Company Limited contact the above address, or visit our website: http://www.helion.co.uk.

We always welcome receiving book proposals from prospective authors.

Contents

Preface v
Foreword vi

1. The Task of the Netherlands Armed Forces 7
2. The Forces at the Disposal of the Kingdom 8
3. The Geographical Character of the Netherlands from the Military Standpoint. 14
4. The Netherlands Plan of Operations 18
5. Considerations in relation to the Netherlands Plan of Operations 23
6. Events shortly before the Outbreak of the Conflict. 27
7. The German Plan of Operations 28
8. The Course of Military Events on the 10th May 30
    The Attack on the Heart of the Country 30
    The Struggle in the Southern Provinces 36
    Events in the Valley Positions, in the Area East of the Latter, and in the Northern Provinces 40
    The Situation at the End of the First Day of War 42
9. The Military Operations on the 11th May 44
    The Fighting in the Heart of the Country and on the Southern Front of the Holland Fortress 44
    The Military Operations in North Brabant. 48
    Events in the Valley Position and in the Northern Provinces. 49
    The Military Position at the End of the Second Day of War 51
10. Military Operations on the 12th May 52
    The Struggle in the Heart of the Country and on the Southern Front of the Holland Fortress 52
    The Military Operations in North Brabant. 53
    The Fighting in the Valley Position and in the Northern Provinces . . . 54
    The Situation at the End of the Third Day of War. 57
11. The Events of the 13th and 14th May 58
    The Fighting in the Valley Position and the Retreat to the East Front of the Holland Fortress 58
    The Military Operations in North Brabant and at the Kornwerderzand . 59
    The Events in the Heart of the Country 60
    The Situation on the Morning of the 14th May, and the Capitulation. . 61
12. The Struggle in Zeeland 63
13. Final Review 65
List of Abbreviations 69

List of Appendices
Appendix I: Distribution of the Principal Dutch Forces over the Various Theatres of Operation 70

Appendix II: Order to the II Battalion of the 65th German Infantry
   Regiment before the Attack on the Hague 75
Appendix III: Radio Speech of the Commander-in-Chief of the Land and
   Sea Forces to the Dutch Nation on the Evening of the 14th May, 1940 . . 78
Appendix IV: Order of the Day of the Dutch Commander-in-Chief of
   Land and Sea Forces of the 15th May, 1940 79

List of Maps
Map No. 1 : Disposition of Dutch Troops on 10th May, 1940 31
Map No. 2: The Attack on the Heart of the Country on the 10th May, 1940 32
Map No. 3: The Fighting in North Brabant on the 10th May, 1940 41
Map No. 4: The Fighting from the 12th to 14th May, 1940 53

Preface

On the occasion of the appearance of this book it is my duty and pleasure to express my thanks to the Netherlands Government Information Bureau, who made its publication possible. In the present difficult circumstances this was in no sense an easy task.

It would scarcely be possible for me to mention by name all the people who have in various ways helped me in the preparation of this book. May I here, then, take this opportunity to thank them collectively.

I must, however, make an exception for Mrs Olive Renier, who not only gave me the utmost assistance as part of her normal work in the Netherlands Government Information Bureau, but who also, outside her official capacity, spared no pains to help me over the many problems which arose.

A few of the photographs reproduced in the book have been taken from illustrations in the Netherlands periodical *De Militaire Spectator*. It was, unfortunately, impossible to obtain permission beforehand for their use. I hope and trust, however, that the editor will forgive me for taking this liberty. The rest of the photographs, however, were supplied by courtesy of the RAF. Nor can I conclude without expressing my gratitude for the whole-hearted co-operation I received from this quarter.

P. L. G. D.

Foreword

The moment has not yet arrived when a complete picture can be given of the events which occurred in Holland during the "Five Days' Campaign." The data which would be required for that purpose, both from Dutch and from German sources, are not available.

If, nevertheless, we endeavour in the following pages to present a brief account of these military operations, it is because it has been repeatedly observed that an erroneous view was widely held with regard to the course of events in that campaign, a view which in many instances has been made the basis of ill-founded criticism.

The pages which follow, therefore, are dedicated to those who, under difficult circumstances, willingly laid down their lives for their country, and to the body of expert military instructors who, in the pre-war years, were called upon to discharge the onerous task of training the Dutch people for the duties of war. These duties, indeed, owing to the long period of peace which had gone before, in which the people had enjoyed to the full the opportunities of cultural development, were particularly difficult.

Finally, they are dedicated to all those in Holland who are dear to us, and who, in these years of stress, are being called upon to suffer for our omissions in the past.

Chapter One

The Task of the Netherlands Armed Forces

On the 13th September, 1938, the Netherlands Minister for Foreign Affairs declared, in the Assembly of the League of Nations, that Holland recognized no obligation, even under Article 16 of the League Covenant, to take part in any common action, or to permit the passage of foreign troops through its territory.

Thus Holland had reverted to the old policy of independence which she followed before 1914.

The object of the Netherlands Government, in issuing this declaration, was to make it manifest to the entire world that in case of any conflict which might possibly arise in the future there was but one attitude to be expected from the Netherlands Government: that of *strict neutrality* towards all belligerents.

This declaration was not, however, in the least meant to imply that the attitude of Holland in a future conflict would be limited to issuing a declaration of neutrality. On the same occasion, indeed, the Minister for Foreign Affairs said: "By arming itself as thoroughly as possible in order, with all the forces at its command, to defend its frontiers against any violation of its integrity, no matter from what quarter, and by thus being able to maintain an armed and effective neutrality, such a state does its national duty, and this attitude will at the same time best serve European interests."

In this way, therefore, the foreign policy of Holland was defined with perfect clarity. At the same time, moreover, the task which the forces at the disposal of the Government of the Netherlands would have to carry out was laid down.

This twofold task consisted of:

(a) Maintenance of Dutch neutrality.
(b) Defence of Dutch independence against any attack from without.

Chapter Two

The Forces at the Disposal of the Kingdom

During the period which immediately followed the world war of 1914–18 the armed forces of Holland fell more or less into a decline. There were two reasons for this. In the first place many sections of the Dutch held over-optimistic views about the newly formed League of Nations and the general disarmament foreshadowed in connection therewith. The second reason was that during the long years of mobilization so many financial and personal burdens had necessarily been shouldered for purposes of defence, that throughout practically the entire nation there was reluctance to face further sacrifices.

The financial crisis during those years was also a contributory factor in reducing expenditure, particularly defence, to the lowest level.

The result of all this was that between 1918 and 1936:

> (a) The strength of the levies was reduced from 23,000 to 19,500; in the period 1920 to 1922 to as little as 13,000 men.
> (b) The cadre of professional officers and non-commissioned officers was cut down considerably.
> (c) Many peacetime formations were abolished.
> (d) The period of first training for unmounted forces was reduced to five and a half months, and in the case of men liable to service, who had already taken part in preliminary military training, to as little as six weeks.
> (e) The most essential supplies of material were neglected, or else were on so modest a scale that whole decades would have been needed for the attainment of anything like tolerable conditions.

Nor was this all. During those years when training and supplies were below reasonable limits, the state of preparedness had also fallen off considerably. The number of peacetime formations was cut down to such an extent that each formation had to be multiplied six or eight times to put it on a wartime basis. Such an expansion could not be carried out all at once. It required an intermediate phase in the form of pre-mobilization, in which the nuclei of the wartime formations had to be created. The general mobilization which followed shortly afterwards then raised the nuclei in question to full war strength. Owing to this fact the entire process of putting the forces on a war footing was prolonged for some days.

In the meantime, circumstances in the world around under-went a complete change.

After power in Germany had passed into the hands of Hitler in 1933, there followed in rapid succession the events the object of which was to unite all German, or presumed German, territories in a "Greater Germany" and to put this state in a position to dominate the Continent.

The year 1935 began with the plebiscite in the Saar territory, as a consequence of which the Saar reverted to Germany.

In March of the same year Germany introduced the militia system, and in doing so threw over one of the most important provisions of the Treaty of Versailles. The return to the militia system meant that within a few years the German armed forces would again have grown to such an extent as to rank among the most powerful in the world.

June witnessed the Naval Treaty with England, while in October of the same year Italy entered on the war against Abyssinia, a war which not only ended with the complete occupation of that territory, but also drew Italy, as a result, into the wake of Germany.

The Franco-Russian pact, concluded in the beginning of 1936, afforded some relief. It looked as if a balance of forces was in process of slowly coming into being on the Continent. The occupation of the Rhineland, however, destroyed any such expectations.

Owing to the possibility of converting her western frontier into a strong wall of defence, Germany was able to provide herself with a defensive flank. This gave her freedom of action in the south and the east. The armies of the Western Powers would now no longer be able, in case of need, to come quickly to the aid of their hard-pressed allies in Central and Eastern Europe. It was once more possible for the German General Staff to operate on internal lines.

In 1938 and 1939 the moment had arrived for Hitler to harvest the crop which had been sown during the preceding years. Austria, the Sudeten territory and later the whole of Czechoslovakia became his victims.

Italy, which had now entirely been absorbed into the orbit of Germany and also wished to gather in her share of the profits, began her operation against Albania in the spring of 1939. Such was the position when, in the autumn of the same year, Hitler prepared for the next coup: the Corridor and Danzig. It was a coup which was to mark the beginning of a new world war.

Apart from the fact that the above events had prompted the Dutch Government to review its entire foreign policy, and, as has already been pointed out, to revert to complete independence, a review of the army policy adopted during the previous years likewise became inevitable.

It was not merely the fact that day by day there was a greater likelihood of events developing in course of time into a military conflict in which Holland might be involved, but new factors emerged as regards the tactics and strategy to be expected in such a conflict.

Among these factors was the appearance of tank troops and motorized units in the organization of the Great Powers surrounding Holland, and also the immense growth of the air force.

Germany in particular, in building up her new armed forces, included a number of armoured and motorized divisions in her organization. These units already possessed a very high degree of military readiness even in peacetime. Consequently the units in question could be called into action and employed in operations within a few hours. The same may be said of the powerful air arm, which was spread over a large number of airfields and was also in perpetual readiness.

If, in the light of these facts, we examine the condition of the Dutch forces (of which, during certain periods of the year, there were practically no trained soldiers at all in the barracks), it becomes clear that such conditions could not be allowed to endure and that, except at the cost of the abandonment of every possibility of successful defence of our territory, a change in the policy so far adopted as regards defence was essential.

This could not be more pointedly expressed than in the words which Minister Colijn addressed in 1936 to the representatives of the people: "We no longer have an army; it will have to be created at the time of mobilization."

In point of fact, having regard to the system then in operation, under which the nuclei of the formations had first to be created during the period of pre-mobilization and then raised to wartime strength during the general mobilization some time later, in order finally, during the period of concentration, to take up their war positions, at least four to five days were needed before the Dutch forces could be ready for fighting. It was clear to all that, under the circumstances then prevailing, there was nothing to justify the belief that Holland would be allowed this period for undisturbed preparation.

In 1936, therefore, there followed the change in the policy of defence, and this change finally received its confirmation in the Military Service Law of 1938.

Under this law:

(a) The strength of the levies was increased by 8,000 men, and thus raised from 19,500 to 27,500 men.

This extension had become essential in order to remedy the extreme anæmia from which the Dutch infantry was suffering.

But an army system requires time to become effective. As the war army was made up of fifteen levies, it would take fifteen years before this increase of strength attained its full effect. It was evident that a period of such length could not be reckoned on. In order to make up to some extent for this difficulty, it was decided that the 1939–43 levies should comprise 5,000 additional men. For those years, therefore, the levies would amount to 32,500 men.

(b) The period of service was fixed at eleven months.

As the infantry came to the colours in two batches every year, and as it may be considered that a soldier is suitable for certain forms of fighting after five months' training, the result of this measure was that one half of the infantry levy was always available as trained troops. From this trained portion of the levy twenty-four frontier battalions were formed. They were stationed close to the main roads into Holland, and their object was to repel an unexpected attack, and in this way to allow the Dutch forces sufficient time to mobilize and concentrate.

The twenty-four battalions in question were, however, not sufficient for the discharge of this duty. Therefore an additional organization was created, by which certain sections could, apart from a general mobilization, be called to the colours separately in order to be available for this strategic measure. These sections also consisted chiefly of infantry units. They, however, likewise included the air force and air defence units. (As these units were called up by means of a telegram with the letter Q, they were everywhere known as Q sections).

FORCES AT THE DISPOSAL OF THE KINGDOM   11

As regards the infantry, the Q sections consisted chiefly of older levies having their place of residence in the frontier territories.

Finally:

(c) A defence fund was formed with the object of making good within the shortest possible time the great deficiency which existed as regards supplies of material.

The period during which the new Military Service Law was in operation before war came was too short to allow of complete success.

Nevertheless its result was that on the second day of Easter 1939 – the day of the Italian attack on Albania – the frontier battalions and the Q sections were able to take up their war positions, in order to safeguard a general mobilization which might take place later. This did not occur till the end of August, however, when the Dutch forces were raised to complete war strength.

In the months September 1939 to May 1940 great efforts were made to improve training and efficiency to the utmost possible extent.

Unfortunately little could be done to make up for the shortage of equipment, the reason being that in this respect Holland was practically dependent on foreign countries. Among other things, the light howitzers ordered in Germany, which were so urgently needed to strengthen the divisional artillery, were only delivered in very small quantities, and even then practically without ammunition.

At the outbreak of the conflict Holland possessed the following armed forces (see also Appendix I):

(a) Four army corps each consisting of:

The staff.

Two infantry divisions, each consisting of the staff, three infantry brigades, one machine-gun company, one regiment divisional artillery, consisting of the staff and three brigades (two brigades armed with field guns of 7 cm and one brigade with 12 cm or 15 cm howitzers) and one company of pioneers.

The army corps troops consisting of:

One regiment of hussars, consisting of the staff, two mounted squadrons, four cyclist squadrons, one machine-gun squadron, one anti-tank squadron, one platoon of mortars, and one platoon of tanks.

One regiment of army corps artillery, but consisting only of one brigade of three batteries armed with 10 cm medium artillery.

The army corps train.

(b) One light division, consisting of the staff, two brigades of cyclists, two regiments of motor cyclist hussars, the corps of horse artillery, consisting of a staff and two brigades of artillery, armed with 7 cm light field guns and the divisional train.

(c) Twenty-four brigades of infantry, made up of the older levies.

These brigades were numbered from 23 to 46 inclusive; part of them were combined into brigade groups.

(d) Twenty-four frontier battalions of infantry.

(e) Fourteen regiments of army artillery. These regiments were, however, to a large extent armed with obsolete material (guns of 8 cm steel, 12 cm length and 15 cm length 24, guns with rigid carriages, without recoil). The Fifteenth Regiment Artillery only was armed with the modern howitzer of 15 cm length 15, and motorized. In the remaining regiments the guns were horse drawn, or else they were entirely non-mobile and could therefore only be used in fixed positions.

(f) A regiment of hussars consisting of the staff and four mounted squadrons.

(g) A number of detachments for the occupation of existing permanent works, and for guarding important objects within the country.

(h) Depot troops.

The brigade of infantry consisted of the staff, three battalions of infantry, one mortar company and one anti-tank company. In all, each infantry battalion had thirty-six light and twelve medium machine guns.

The infantry division, therefore, in the main possessed guns as follows:

9 x 36 = 324 light machine guns.
9 x 12 +18 = 126 medium machine guns.
3 x 12 = 36 anti-tank guns (the companies were, however, not yet at full strength).
3 x 6 = 18 mortars of 8 cm (3-inch mortars).
2 x 12 = 24 7 cm light field guns.
1 x 12 = 12 howitzers of 12 cm length 14, or 15 cm length 17.

As regards the Air Force, there was one bomber squadron, one squadron for strategic reconnaissance and four squadrons of fighter aircraft. In addition the organization included five squadrons intended to co-operate directly with the ground forces.

The anti-aircraft defences consisted of a moderate number of batteries armed with modern weapons, Vickers and Bofors, supplemented by a number of batteries armed with fairly obsolete guns. In addition the organization included a number of independent platoons of anti-aircraft machine gunners. A number of these were combined into companies, allocated to the big units. Others were allotted the task of guarding important objectives in the interior.

If we consider the composition of the Dutch forces with a critical eye, the weak points necessarily strike us at once.

We may mention the following as the chief among them:

(a) Insufficient artillery power.

The division with an infantry strength of nine battalions possessed only thirty-six guns, which were in addition not quite modern. The army corps artillery proper numbered only twelve guns.

Altogether the army corps, with an organic strength of eighteen battalions of infantry only, had seven brigades of artillery – that is to say, about one-half of what is adopted as the normal in foreign organizations. True there were fourteen regiments of army artillery, but their weapons were so much out of date that, though they could be used on less important parts of the front, they were quite unable to provide the necessary artillery support at decisive points.

(b) Insufficient anti-tank weapons.

In the organization of each brigade of infantry or cavalry regiment there was only one anti-tank unit, and even this unit was armed with only a few guns.

(c) Entirely inadequate anti-aircraft defence.

In small countries, the air force of which cannot be expected, in the long run, to maintain a fight with the air forces of great powers, it is essential in particular that the ground anti-aircraft defences shall not only be of specially great relative strength, but that they shall also be perfectly armed. In the Dutch forces neither of these conditions was fulfilled.

(d) Insufficient training of personnel.

The majority of the levies had only completed a first period of training, varying from five and a half months to six weeks, while in the years which followed repeat drill had only been practised for a short time and only once or twice. Owing to these circumstances manoeuvres on a large scale could only be held sporadically.

It need hardly be said that the Dutch Army Command were acutely aware of these weak points.

The circumstances to which the inadequate equipment of the forces was due have already been pointed out, with the added fact that when at last this inadequacy was generally recognized there was no time to make good the deficiencies.

Only the insufficiency of training could to some extent be remedied during the period between September 1939 and the outbreak of hostilities in May 1940.

Notwithstanding all these deficiencies the Dutch armed forces were, when the conflict broke out, from the highest to the lowest, ready to devote themselves with complete self-sacrifice to the lofty task which awaited them.

Chapter Three

The Geographical Character of the Netherlands from the Military Standpoint

(See Map 1)

Holland belongs almost in its entirety to the basin of the great rivers, the Meuse and the Rhine.

As regards the southern portion of the country, the high-lying ground is south of the line Bergen op Zoom-Roosendaal-Breda-'s Hertogenbosch-Ravestein. The land here consists, however, of alternative heath and woodland, containing a number of clearings and settlements. Yet, generally speaking, this territory is far from presenting clear and open spaces, and it is therefore not very well adapted for military operations. On the border between Brabant and Limburg lies the entirely open area of the Peel. This was originally marshland, but the peat moor area has been partly cleared. Still, the land, off the roads, continues even now to be impassable for large masses of troops.

In Limburg the hilly land approaches very close to the Meuse at various points, the east bank of which is usually on a higher level than the west.

South Limburg proper, an important Dutch industrial area, and the only place in Holland where coal is mined, is particularly hilly. The river Geul which cuts through this area is for the most part deep, but otherwise is not in any sense a considerable military obstacle.

From the east there are a considerable number of roads running through Dutch territory to Belgium, but only four of them pass over the Meuse by means of bridges – namely, at Maastricht, Roosteren, Roermond and Venlo.

From east to west the following continuous waterways are met with successively in the southern provinces, in the direction south to north:

> (a) The Meuse, duplicated at some points by the Juliana Canal. The Meuse, especially since it has been canalized by dams, has become a waterway of great military importance. A drawback, however, is that it lies only a few kilometres from the German frontier, and that at various points the west bank is dominated by the east bank.

> (b) The Noorder Canal, joining on to the Peel area, and prolonged northwards by the Raam.

The first-named canal is narrow and runs in part through wooded land. The Raam is not an obstacle of any importance, especially in its southern part, but the strength of this river for purposes of resistance can be increased at various points by means of flooding.

GEOGRAPHICAL CHARACTER OF THE NETHERLANDS 15

(c) The Zuid Willemsvaart.

The canal has high dykes on both sides, while shrubland and inhabited areas extend over great distances along the banks. For this reason it is not very well adapted for a pro-longed defence.

(d) The Dommel.

(e) The Mark.

The two small rivers last mentioned are of practically no importance as obstacles, and in addition they run to a great extent through woodland and inhabited places.

Finally, there is a waterline from east to west in the form of the Wilhelmina Canal, running from Beek-en-Donk through Tilburg and Oosterhout to Geertruidenberg.

The area lying north of the high land of Brabant and south of the Meuse, especially north and northeast of 's Hertogenbosch, is entirely open. Only the Langstraat presents a narrow strip of groups of villages forming an almost uninterrupted line.

The territory lying between the rivers Meuse and Waal, and between the Waal and Lek, is generally speaking very open. Only the orchards, during certain seasons of the year, provide some cover against visibility from the air. The dykes along the river are high, while the roads generally speaking are narrow, stand out sharply and for the most part are located on the open dykes.

Permanent bridges pass over the Meuse at Grave, Hedel, Heusden and the Keizersveer. Over the Waal, on the contrary, the only bridges are at Nijmegen and Zalt-Bommel, while the only bridges over the Lek are at Arnhem, Culemborg and Vianen.

The rivers are some hundreds of metres wide, and the rate of flow is such as to make crossing in small assault barges difficult.

The territory of Holland proper (the provinces of North and South Holland) lying north of the river area and west of the line Wijk bij Duurstede-Utrecht-Naarden, is a very open polder area intersected by innumerable ditches, channels and canals. The roads are generally open. Only along the coast, beginning at The Hague, and extending as far as the sea dyke at Petten, is there an area of dunes having a width of some kilometres. The approaches from the sea at the Hook of Holland and Ymuiden, and also the naval bases at Den Helder, call for special attention from the military point of view.

Furthermore, the banks of the Ysselmeer, with the ports of Medemblik, Enkhuizen, Hoorn, Edam, Volendam and Amsterdam, constitute a gateway of attack for an enemy who has conquered Friesland, Overyssel or Gelderland, and is able from there to command the Ysselmeer.

South of the Nieuwe Waterweg extends the island territory of South Holland and Zeeland.

These islands also are quite open. They, however, possess passive security in the great rivers and arms of the sea which wash their shores.

The chief island in this territory is Walcheren, both because the approach to Antwerp is controlled from that point, and because Flushing is a seaport of some importance.

South Beveland is joined to the mainland of North Brabant by means of a dam, with adjoining polders, while between Walcheren and South Beveland there is the Sloedam.

South Beveland itself is intersected by the Hansweerd Wemeldinge canal, which canal, however, owing to the high dykes and the built-up areas around, is less suitable for a prolonged defence than the territory farther eastward at the Zanddijk, where the possibility of flooding may render an approach from the east exceedingly difficult.

Likewise the land at Bath, the most easterly portion of South Beveland, forms a strong natural obstacle.

The eastern part of Utrecht and the Veluwe consists of undulating hilly ground. Extensive forests alternate with large open areas of heath and sand drifts.

Between both these areas is the Gelder Valley, constituting the basin of the Eem and the Grift. This area also, in which extensive portions can be flooded, especially in the north, has natural defences of great strength.

The basin of the Yssel extends from Arnhem to Kampen. In the southern portion the high lands of the Veluwe approach very closely to the river, so that there the west bank dominates the east bank, which fact is very favourable to defence on an eastern front.

Further to the north the land is flat, and the river there is surrounded by high dykes.

The river itself is of considerable width, and for that reason has great natural strength. Bridges connect the two banks at Arnhem, Doesburg, Zutphen, Deventer and Zwolle.

The Spankeren-Apeldoorn-Hattem-Zwolle canal is of little military importance. It is narrow and runs for a great deal of its length through wooded land and built-up areas, while in addition a destruction of the lock at Spankeren would drain the canal in some places.

The land lying east of the Yssel is very well adapted for an advance from an easterly direction. The waterways in this region flow from east to west, so that a continuous waterline in the direction south to north is not met with anywhere. The ground, therefore, is not very suitable for delaying actions. The Deventer-Raalte-Lemelerveld canal might be of some importance for this purpose, but it lies outside the most obvious line of advance for an opponent coming from the east.

The Twente canals also run from east to west, so that these again are of little importance for the defence of the country.

The northerly provinces, as cattle-raising, agricultural and industrial regions, are of particular value in the defence of the country. Apart from the high land in Drente, the soil for the most part consists of peat land and clay. Thus, along the eastern border, from Gramsbergen, by way of Coevorden, Ter Apel and Stadskanaal, a peat area extends, intersected by ditches, channels and canals, and this is a kind of land which is very well adapted for delaying actions. Winschoten commands the whole of East Groningen as a bastion.

Finally in Friesland, entirely open, a natural line of defence is encountered in the old Frisian line of lakes extending from Sloten to east of Leeuwarden. The clay land lying north of this, however, affords a very good passage for troops and would require a very large number of men for prolonged defence.

Another important point for the defence of the country in this region is Zurig, the place where the outer dyke of the Zuider Zee which runs from the Province of Holland to Friesland reaches the coast.

Chapter Four
The Netherlands Plan of Operations
(See Map 1)

The task which the Dutch forces would have to fulfil in case of a conflict was clearly defined by the foreign policy which had been specifically laid down – namely:
Maintenance of neutrality.
Defence of the territory against any act of aggression.

Maintenance of neutrality meant that at every point on the frontiers of the territory forces had to be present or at least available for being brought up speedily, in order to repulse those who might violate the country's neutrality. In practice, therefore, troops had to be maintained for this purpose at all important points on the frontiers or on the lengthy coastline. Frontier and coastguards, supplemented by naval and air patrols, played the chief part in carrying out this duty.

The defence of the territory, really the principal task, made quite different demands, however.

Of necessity the aim was to defend every part of Dutch territory, as was in truth repeatedly declared by various Ministers at the assemblies of the States General.

But the Dutch frontier is not only long – the eastern frontier alone, from Vaals to the Dollard, measured as the crow flies, has a length of about 400 km – but, as has already been stated, the nature of the ground, owing to the absence of any natural obstacles, is such that lengthy portions are not in the least suited for prolonged defence. The same applies to the southern frontier, which has a length of fully 300 km, likewise without any natural protection.

Even the waterway which would rank in the first place for a continuous line of defence with the eastern front – namely, the Meuse and Yssel with the Meuse-Waal canal lying between – has a length of fully 400 km., which means that a stubborn defence would require a number of troops exceeding many times that of the Dutch forces. Even the defence of the part of the Yssel between Arnhem and Kampen, with a length of 70 km, is a task beyond the powers of the forces available.

Therefore the Dutch Army Command had necessarily to confine itself to the heart of the country, as regards continuous defence of the territory.

Even in the past a line had been constructed for this purpose, the "New Holland Waterline," later called the East Front of the Holland Fortress, along the line (from north to south) Muiden-Weesp-Breukelen, and then to the east of the town of Utrecht. Thereupon the line followed Schalkwijk-Leerdam-Gorinchem, where support in the south was provided by the water area of the Biesbosch, the Hollandsch Diep and the Haringvliet (south front of the Holland Fortress).

The great strength of this line was derived from the fact that, as regards the chief zone of resistance, flooding could be effected to a width of 1 to 5 km over its entire length, except for a portion at Utrecht. The entire zone was provided with permanent defensive works, which were, however, to a large extent obsolete in their construction. Nevertheless, great value was still attached to these works as points of infantry support, owing to the large surface, the massive earthworks, and the safety against attack provided by the presence of wide, wet ditches. This was particularly true where, as was the case at various points, modern casemates had been built into these earthworks. Such casemates were also constructed at all points where roads traversed the area of the position.

The length of the east front of the Holland Fortress was about 60 km. Allowing for the number of natural obstacles in the region, the defence of this position did not exceed the powers of the Dutch forces.

Nevertheless, the position was not without its drawbacks. Among these the following must be mentioned:

> (a) The fact that the high ground in the eastern part of the province of Utrecht would have to be yielded up to the enemy, which gave him the possibility not only of finding covered positions, but positions which dominated the actual zone of resistance.
>
> (b) The growing strength of modern artillery fire and air bombing.
>
> In most instances, too, the floods on our own side ended against dykes and quays. In the first place this compelled the defender, if he wanted to have a field of fire, to take up linear positions on the dykes. Moreover, a disadvantage of these dykes was the risk that heavy bombardment would destroy them, thus inundating our own positions.
>
> (c) The city of Utrecht, in which the built-up areas approached very closely to the position, was a drawback to the defence, lying as it did in the centre of the east front.
>
> (d) The impossibility of ever making contact by land with possible allies. The broad river area in the south formed an absolutely insuperable obstacle to all who might have been able to render help.
>
> (e) The impossibility of our ever breaking out ourselves from behind the wide floods.

In view of the foregoing considerations, the attention of Army Command in the years preceding the war had been directed more and more to the Valley position.

This position, too, which runs from north to south, from Eemnes eastward by way of Amersfoort, thence along the line Woudenberg-Veenendaal-Rhenen, possesses great natural strength, because in several places, especially in the northern part, flooding can be effected.

Furthermore, the high ground in the eastern part of the province of Utrecht would now be on our own side, and as a result the position would at several points dominate the ground on the east front.

This position has an advantage over that of the east front of the Holland Fortress: it allows for the covered construction of defences in depth and the concentration of reserves.

The length, from the Ysselmeer to Rhenen, is not more than 40 km., so that a prolonged defence of this position was not beyond the powers of the Dutch forces.

An opportunity for breaking out was provided along the parts remaining dry in the flooded area, while by an extension through the area lying between the Meuse and the Lek, along the line Rhenen-Apeltern, contact could be made with the Dutch and possibly the Allied forces present in North Brabant.

On the basis of all these considerations the Dutch Army Command decided to select the Valley position as the line in which the Dutch forces should carry on the main defence.

During the last years preceding the war, the natural strength of this line was increased to the utmost limit by the construction of a large number of casemates and steel cupolaed bunkers. A ditch extending the whole length of the position likewise provided it with the necessary defence against tanks.

In addition to defence along this line, for reasons already stated – the safeguarding of mobilization and concentration – an enemy advance would be delayed in the outer provinces.

Particular value was attached to this delay, which Army Command pictured as taking place in the east of North Brabant.

If the situation in Brabant is viewed in connection with what happened as regards territorial defence in Belgium, one is struck by the fact that Weert, the southern wing point of the link formed by the Raam, the Peel region and the Noorder Canal, lies only 40 km from Hasselt, on the Albert Canal.

Although the policy of strict neutrality adopted by Holland excluded the possibility of any contact being made with foreign powers with regard to contemplated military preparations, Army Command nevertheless had to take into account the possibility that Holland and Belgium would simultaneously be involved in a conflict with Germany. It was important in this connection to examine what were the theoretical possibilities open to the Belgian Army Command in such a case.

Having regard to the nature of the land, these were found to be the following:

(1) The Belgian forces would maintain a persistent defence on the Meuse as far as Liége, and this defence would be extended to the north along the Belgian Zuid-Willemsvaart.

In such a case the Belgian defence front could join up with the Dutch at Weert.

(2) The Belgian forces would extend the Meuse defence to the north, as indicated under (1), along the Albert Canal, ending at the wing point of Antwerp.

In this case a few divisions interposed between Hasselt and Weert would also be able to maintain a continuous defence.

(3) The Belgian principal defence would be conducted on the Meuse as far as Namur and from that point by way of Louvain to Antwerp.

In this latter case the south wing of the Raam-Peel position at Weert would be liable to be outflanked.

NETHERLANDS PLAN OF OPERATIONS

What the Belgian Army Command contemplated doing was not known to the Dutch General Staff. In the preparation for defence of their own territory, however, it was obvious that the above possibilities had to be taken into account. Therefore particular attention was paid to the development of the Raam-Peel position. At first designed as a purely delaying line, the possibility that the line might be persistently defended was later envisaged.

Therefore, the Dutch plan of operations, as regards an attack from the east, comprised:

(a) Delaying an enemy advance in the territory east of the Yssel (chiefly for the purpose of covering the destruction to be carried out in this area).

(b) Delaying an enemy advance along the line the Meuse-Meuse-Waal canal-Yssel.

(c) Delaying an enemy advance in the position Raam-Peel with the possibility of changing these delaying tactics into a persistent defence, depending on what might be done by possible allies.

(d) Persistent defence of the Valley position extended through the area between the Lek and the Meuse, and afterwards along the Meuse in order to join up at Grave with the Raam-Peel position.

Further:

(e) Delaying an enemy advance in the sense indicated under (a) in the territory of South Limburg, lying east of the Meuse.

(f) Delaying an enemy advance (on the east canal front) in the northerly provinces, and persistent defence of the head of the outer dyke of the Zuider Zee.

Delaying action on the lines mentioned under (b) and (c) was prepared in such a manner that a continuous firing front was secured by guns set up in casemates or steel cupolaed bunkers.

As regards the lines mentioned under (e) and (f) there were casemates at the chief passages over canals or approach roads.

On the basis of this plan of operations, on the 10th May, the day on which the conflict broke out, the Dutch forces were disposed as indicated on Map 1.

When considering this disposition the following should be noted:

Until shortly before the moment when the conflict broke out the Raam-Peel position was occupied by the Third Army Corps and the Peel division, while, in order to cover the open south wing at Weert, the Light Division was disposed to the rear in echelons.

With this disposition of troops in the Raam-Peel position, therefore, defence was the foremost object. True, the length of the Raam-Peel position between Weert and Grave was still quite 60 km – that is to say, one which far exceeds the powers of defence of three divisions under normal conditions – but it must be borne in mind that the entire middle section of the Raam-Peel position, extending between Mill and Nederweert – that is to say, a section of about 45 km – is naturally so strong that weak forces may suffice for the defence of the approaches traversing this territory. Therefore, the strength of the defence could be concentrated on the Mill-Grave part, where at the outset the main body of the Third Army Corps was disposed.

A few days before the outbreak of the conflict the Dutch Supreme Command realized that only a few weak sections of the Belgian forces were on the Zuid Willemsvaart, so that, in case of an attack from the east, the resistance on the said canal would presumably only be of short duration. It could likewise not be regarded as probable that Allied forces could arrive in time to close the gap south of Weert. Therefore, the Commander-in-Chief of the Land and Sea Forces decided to adopt only delaying tactics in the Raam-Peel position.

The Third Army Corps and the Light Division had now as a matter of course to be allocated to the defence of the south river front, and in case of necessity as reserve for the occupation of the Valley position. With this in view the Third Army Corps was withdrawn, leaving a few battalions in the Raam-Peel position, and was concentrated in the region shown on the map. If an attack really took place from the east, this army corps would take up a position behind the Waal, in the space between Ochten and Gorinchem, while the Light Division would be transferred to the environs of Rotterdam.

Obviously, it would have been possible to get the units in question to carry out the necessary displacements for this purpose at once. The reason why this was not done was that it was thought desirable:

>(a) To leave an enemy in uncertainty as long as possible with regard to the resistance to be expected in North Brabant.

>(b) For reasons connected with neutrality, to maintain a considerable force as long as possible south of the big rivers.

The task of the First Army Corps, depending on the circumstances, was:

>(a) Defence of the coast front.

>(b) To form the reserve for the occupation of the Valley position.

>(c) Occupation of the most important parts of the east front of the Holland Fortress, which was itself the second line of defence.

For the rest the most important parts of the fronts of the Holland Fortress were occupied by guard detachments consisting of infantry troops, strengthened at some points by brigades of artillery, all of which were, however, armed with out-of-date weapons.

The Ysselmeer itself was guarded by a small flotilla consisting of a few armoured boats, mine sweepers, one torpedo boat and a number of motor boats.

Chapter Five

Considerations in Relation to the Netherlands Plan of Operations

(See Map 1, Appendix I)

If we examine the disposition of the Dutch forces on the eve of the outbreak of the conflict, it is evident that this disposition, in consequence of the attitude of strict neutrality adopted by the Government, was intended to allow for all possibilities which might arise.

An attack from the east, apart from the delaying actions on the lines mentioned, would be held in the Valley position, while in that case the Third Army Corps, by occupying the Waal front, would create a continuous defence with the south front of the Holland Fortress. The First Army Corps and also the Light Division would finally form the reserve at the disposal of the Chief Command.

If an attack took place from a southerly direction, it would, after being delayed in North Brabant, particularly on the Wilhelmina Canal, be held on the Waal and the south front of the Holland Fortress. In addition to the troops of the Third Army Corps available for this purpose, and the sections belonging to the security garrison of the Holland Fortress, there could also be employed for this defence the First Army Corps and also units from the Valley position, which position under these circumstances would no longer be important.

From a westerly direction, an attack would be held on the coast by the security garrison of the west front of the Holland Fortress, the First Army Corps, the troops in Zeeland, and those occupying the position of Den Helder, while in these circumstances the whole of the forces occupying the Valley position and the troops in North Brabant could strengthen this defence in a later phase.

The disposition was therefore designed to meet the task imposed on the Dutch Supreme Command by the foreign policy of Holland. The question must, however, now be put whether this disposition was also in keeping with the principle generally applied in strategy of the economy of forces. In dealing with this question we will confine ourselves to the case which actually occurred – namely, an attack from the east.

It is particularly desirable to examine whether there were not too many forces allocated to subsidiary strategic functions, forces which in the final outcome would cease to be available for the main struggle, for which in the nature of things there never can be sufficient strength.

Let us examine the distribution of forces a little more closely in this connection.

24 MILITARY OPERATIONS OF THE DUTCH ARMY

As has already been stated, the total forces available were:

	Battalions
24 brigades of infantry of the field army	72
24 brigades of infantry, ie numbers 23 to 46 inclusive	72
24 frontier battalions	24
2 brigades of cyclists	6
5 regiments of hussars, amounting to	5
2 regiments of hussar motor-cyclists, amounting to	2
In all a force of	181

These forces, in case of an attack from the east, were allocated as follows:

		Battalions
(a)	Delaying action east of the Yssel	5
(b)	Territorial defence of South Limburg	4
(c)	Ditto Northern Provinces	7
(d)	Delaying action on river line Meuse-Yssel	16
(e)	Delaying action in south part of North Brabant	3
(f)	Territorial defence of Zeeland	4
(g)	Delaying action in the Raam-Peel position	14
	Total for subsidiary strategic tasks	53

		Battalions
(h)	As guard security garrisons on the fronts of the Holland Fortress and in occupation of important objects in the interior	32
(i)	Defence of the Valley position, a strength of	39
(j)	Defence of the region between the Meuse and the Lek	12
(k)	Defence of the Waal, to the south front of the Holland Fortress (those troops withdrawn from the Third Army Corps and the Light Division)	26
(l)	General reserve (First Army Corps) a strength of	19
	Total strength for the principal action	96

If we reckon that the troops mentioned under (e) in the case of attack from the east would be allocated for defence of the south front of the Holland Fortress, the figure for the respective duties becomes 50-32-99.

For the performance of the principal task, the defence of the heart of the country, fully one-half of the available forces were therefore allocated.

The allocation of a fighting strength of fifty battalions, quite one-fourth of the total available forces, for the performance of strategically subsidiary tasks appears high.

Let us examine, therefore, to what extent the distribution and allocation of the troops in each of the territories mentioned was strategically justified.

(a) The troops intended for delaying action east of the Yssel were chiefly meant to safeguard the work of destruction which had been prepared there. A figure of five battalions for an area fully 100 km in length, with a depth varying from 20 to 60 km., is certainly not too high for this.

(b) South Limburg is an area of great political importance. If only for that reason it would have been inadmissible to leave this part of the country entirely undefended and open for a German advance against the Belgian system of defence. The allocation of four battalions to this duty is certainly a minimum.

(c) The northern provinces, as has been said above, were of great economic importance for the conduct of war. The fundamental idea which gave rise to the decision to defend this area territorially was that an opponent must be prevented from occupying these provinces with very weak forces. If an opponent knew that in order to conquer them considerable forces – or, to put it more definitely, from one to two divisions – were needed, there was the possibility that he would refrain from attacking this territory. And if there were such an attack, the forces engaged there would in any case be drawn from the troops which had to fight the decisive action on the chief centre of operations, and this would indirectly benefit the main Dutch defence or our allies.

Territorial defence of the northern provinces was therefore strategically fully justified. In view of the extent of the territory the number of battalions allotted was essential.

(d) As regards the troops intended for delaying action on the river line Meuse-Yssel, it must be recalled that originally the reason for the intended delaying tactics on this line was to give the main body of the forces the opportunity of mobilizing and concentrating. This reason, however, was no longer operative, since the Dutch forces had in September 1939 carried out mobilization and taken up war positions without hindrance by enemy action. Nevertheless, the idea of delaying action on this line was adhered to in order to give the units in the principal defence some time to attain complete readiness for action. The lack of depth of Dutch territory, together with the great mobility of German motorized units, rendered this necessary.

If delaying tactics are to be at all effective the very least which must be demanded is that a continuous firing front can be formed. From Roermond to Zwolle the length of this line is about 180 km. If it was held by sixteen battalions, therefore, each battalion would have charge of a length of 10 to 15 km. Any further dilution of this cordon disposition would have made the entire resistance worthless, because it would then have been a very simple matter to roll it up. When once delaying tactics had been decided upon, therefore, the number of sixteen battalions could not be reduced.

(e) The battalions intended for delaying action in the southern part of North Brabant were, in case of an attack from the east, to be allocated to the defence of the southern front of the Holland Fortress, and therefore can be left out of account.

(f) With respect to Zeeland, it was essential in all circumstances to prevent an important port, such as Flushing, being captured by an enemy by surprise. Therefore, there was un-questionable justification for the battalions allocated to the defence of this territory.

(g) Delaying action in the Raam-Peel position was strategically justified with a view to the possibility of support being obtained from possible allies. The presence of Franco-British forces in northern France made this a possibility.

In order to reach North Brabant, those units would have had to cover distances of about 200 km, which requires a time of one to two days.

Therefore, the longer the troops in the Raam-Peel position could hold up an enemy advance from the east, the more likelihood was there that the Allied troops would reach North Brabant in time, and the farther east would be the point at which they would perhaps be able to bring an enemy advance to a standstill.

Every hour of additional delay might lead to the result that a larger portion of North Brabant remained in our hands. This consideration was well worth the allocation of fourteen battalions to the Raam-Peel position.

(h) Finally, the strength of thirty-two battalions as security guard for the Holland Fortress, and for the interior, must be considered as a minimum. In particular the anticipated use of air-borne infantry and paratroops made it absolutely essential to retain a considerable number of troops in the interior for the defence of vital points. The story of the campaign proves in actual fact that the number of battalions allotted for this purpose was itself very far from sufficient.

Therefore, the disposition and the distribution of the Dutch forces at the outbreak of the conflict can be fully justified.

Chapter Six

Events shortly before the outbreak of the Conflict

The Dutch Supreme Command necessarily possessed some data concerning the strength of the German forces posted on the Dutch eastern frontier. Shortly before the outbreak of the conflict it was estimated that there were:

(a) On the Dutch frontier in the territory north of the Rhine about ten German divisions.

(b) On the Dutch frontier in the territory between Cleves and the line Munich-Gladbach-Düsseldorf about nine divisions.

(c) Facing South Limburg in the area south of the line mentioned under (b) and Monschau about thirty divisions.

From this disposition of troops it could be inferred that if an attack was to take place from an easterly direction, it would presumably occur along the following axes:

(1) A drive against the heart of the country in the territory north of the great rivers, with subsidiary action, perhaps, against the northern provinces and the outer dyke of the Zuider Zee.

(2) A drive through North Limburg and the eastern part of North Brabant, directed against the Belgian positions on the Albert Canal, west of Hasselt, and perhaps also against the westerly part of North Brabant and Zeeland. It was to be expected that this drive would take place north and south along the Peel territory.

(3) A main attack against the Belgian defensive system on the Meuse and the Albert Canal, south and north of Liége respectively. The northern axis of this attack would presumably run through the southern portion of the Dutch province of Limburg.

Periods of tension had already occurred several times during the winter of 1939–40, and had rendered it necessary to issue further standby orders. Such a crisis occurred again on the 7th May. On that date, therefore, all leave (the ordinary periodical leaves and the longer periods of leave given for purposes of business and study) was cancelled, and at the same time order was given that all frontier and coast troops were to occupy their fighting positions in full strength.

The result of this was that the strategic surprise at which the Germans aimed by their sudden attack on Holland on the morning of the 10th May was unsuccessful.

Chapter Seven
The German Plan of Operations

In the eyes of the German Command Holland was a subsidiary field of operations.

Nevertheless, it was of the utmost importance for that command to occupy Holland as rapidly as possible when attacking in the west, in order to be covered on the right flank in the operations against Belgium and France. Therefore, the forces employed against Holland were considerable.

The German Eighteenth Army, which was to carry out the attack on Holland, comprised the following forces:

> About five infantry divisions
>
> One tank division
>
> One cavalry division
>
> The Twenty-Second Airborne Division
>
> The Second Regiment of Paratroops
>
> The Seventh Air Division,
>
> in addition to the necessary auxiliary troops.
>
> The entire force was under the command of General von Kuchler.

The German plan of attack comprised:

> (a) An attack by air-borne infantry and paratroops on the heart of the country, in order, if possible, to seize the centre of Government on the very first day of the war, and in this way to paralyze the entire resistance (see Appendix II).
>
> (b) An attack on the Valley position and the east front of the Holland Fortress along the axis Arnhem-Rhenen-Utrecht.
>
> (c) An attack through North Brabant with the intention of pushing on as quickly as possible through Moerdijk-Dordrecht-Rotterdam, in order to make contact with the air-borne troops to be landed there.
>
> (d) A subsidiary attack for the purpose of seizing the northern provinces and the Zuider Zee dyke, in order to penetrate into the Holland Fortress by this way also.

Strategically, therefore, the operation presented the aspect of a frontal attack combined with double outflanking, while the air-borne infantry together with the paratroops were to give the stab in the back.

It would be of the utmost importance, especially if the attack mentioned under (a) did not attain the desired success, that the troops operating in North Brabant should make contact as rapidly as possible with the air-borne infantry to be landed at Moerdijk, Dordrecht and in the environs of Rotterdam.

The German commander expected that this attacking group would have to overcome the following resistances:

1. The obstructions east of the Meuse.

2. The Meuse itself.

3. The Raam-Peel position.

4. The Zuid Willemsvaart, and also

5. The Wilhelmina Canal.

Great rapidity of operation was therefore particularly desirable in the southern outflanking group.

Chapter Eight

The Course of Military Events on the 10th May

(See Maps 1, 2, and 3)

1. The Attack on the Heart of the Country.

On the evening of the 9th May, headquarters had already received reports from various quarters, from which it was to be inferred that an attack on the early morning of the 10th May was highly probable. Then shortly after midnight reports came to hand from the aircraft spotters of great German air activity, practically over the entire territory of Holland.

The question whether an air attack on England was contemplated or whether this activity was the first phase of an attack on Holland was speedily settled, when reports were received of air attacks on the airfields of Schiphol, Bergen, Waalhaven, de Kooy, Soesterberg, Haamstede and Hilversum. In addition, a number of the aircraft dropped mines in the outlets to the sea along the Dutch coast, in order to prevent Dutch ships from running out and the possible arrival of help from allies.

With the object of frightfulness, and in order to create confusion from the very outset at the centre of Government, at 5 o'clock and at 10 o'clock air raids were carried out on The Hague.

The Dutch air forces, which had, since the early morning hours been in a state of complete readiness for action, took to the air wherever possible for their struggle against the overpoweringly strong enemy. They succeeded in bringing down a large number of German machines, but their own losses were necessarily heavy. The Dutch anti-aircraft artillery also exacted a heavy toll at the outset from the attacking German aircraft.

Three hours after the air raids had begun, however, the German Ambassador handed a note to the Dutch Government suggesting that all resistance should cease at once.

The Dutch Government, of course, rejected this suggestion, and declared that, by reason of the German attacks which were taking place, a state of war existed between Holland and Germany.

More serious than the air bombings themselves was the fact that paratroops were dropped at various points in the heart of Holland, and succeeded in obtaining control of a few airfields, in consequence of which German air-borne infantry could be landed from transport aircraft.

Thus, the garrison of the Valkenburg airfield, consisting of parts of the Third Battalion, Fourth Infantry Brigade, was, after air bombing at 3.30 am, partly destroyed by paratroops, while the rest of the garrison was forced to retreat. At 7.30 am this airfield was in German hands, and from that moment onwards German reserves were continually brought up by Junkers transport aircraft.

COURSE OF MILITARY EVENTS ON THE 10TH MAY 31

Map 1   DISPOSITION OF NETHERLANDS TROOPS
on the morning of 10th May 1940.

Map No. 1: Disposition of Dutch Troops on 10th May, 1940

Likewise the garrison of the Ypenberg airfield, consisting of the Third Battalion, Brigade of Grenadiers, was forced to evacuate the airfield, and the airfield of Ockenburg, where the garrison were taken by surprise, also fell into German hands. At 6 am this airfield was already occupied by 600 of the enemy.

In addition to the airfields mentioned above, swarms of paratroops were landed near the Maaldrift, in the environs of Wassenaar, on the southern bank of the Meuse at Rotterdam, near Dordrecht and Wieldrecht near the Moerdijk, in the Westland, near Katwijk Binnen, and the Staalduinen.

Map 2

THE ATTACK ON THE HEART OF HOLLAND
on 10th of May 1940.

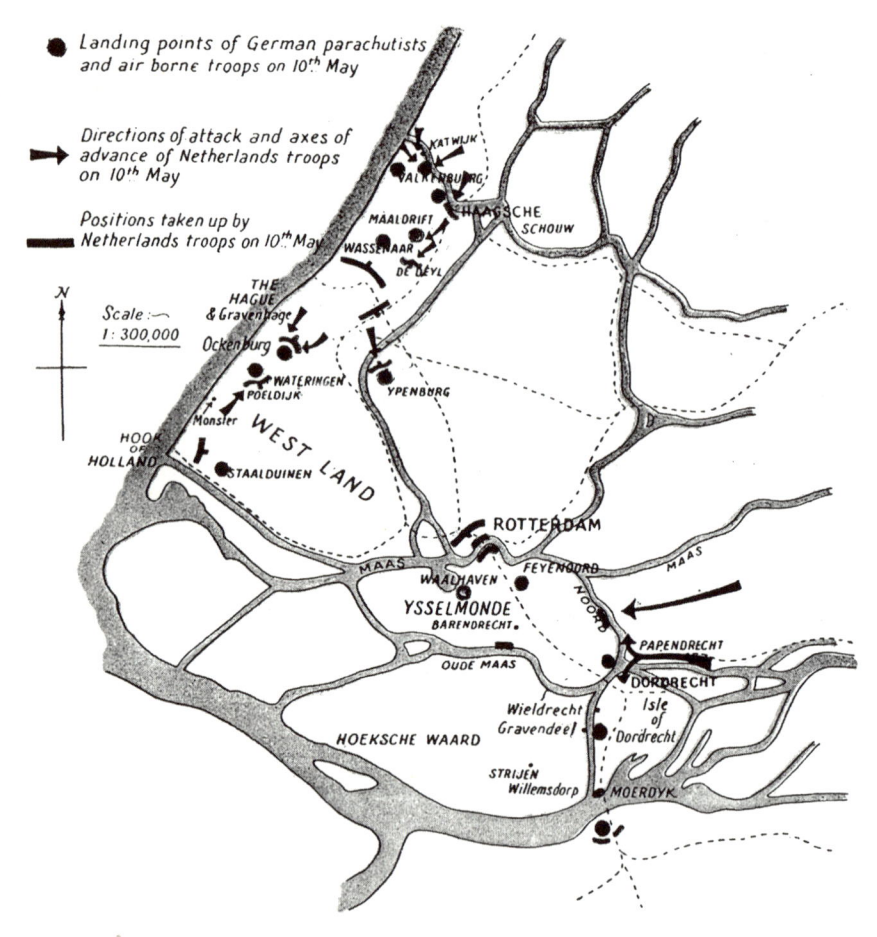

- ● Landing points of German parachutists and air borne troops on 10th May
- ➤ Directions of attack and axes of advance of Netherlands troops on 10th May
- ▬ Positions taken up by Netherlands troops on 10th May

Scale :—
1 : 300,000

Map No. 2: The Attack on the Heart of the Country on the 10th May, 1940

At Rotterdam particularly, where the Germans were assisted by a strong fifth column, consisting of the big German colony living in Rotterdam and a few Dutch traitors, the position was serious. The Germans succeeded in gaining possession of the two bridges over the Meuse and also the bridge over the Oude Maas. The whole of Feyenoord and also the airfield of Waalhaven thus fell into German hands. Rotterdam, as a supply depot, only had a very small garrison. Notwithstanding the efforts made, in which a detachment of marines distinguished themselves, the Dutch troops did not succeed in regaining the bridges over the Meuse.

Torpedo boat Z5, and also the torpedo motor boat 51, both on guard at the Hook of Holland, steamed up the Niieuwe Waterweg, and took part in the artillery

COURSE OF MILITARY EVENTS ON THE 10TH MAY

action against the German forces at Feyenoord, until the war vessels in question had used up the whole of their ammunition.

Besides this, the Netherlands naval vessel Van Galen was summoned from Den Helder to take part in the fighting at Rotterdam.

Although destroyers are necessarily not quite suitable for this sort of action, the ship directed artillery fire on to the airfield of Waalhaven, but was finally destroyed by repeated German air attacks.

The Germans also succeeded in gaining possession, by means of surprise, and with the help of traitors, of the two bridges over the Moerdijk. In this way, in the early morning of the 10th May, the island of Ysselmonde and also a large portion of the island of Dordrecht were in enemy hands, while the troops landed around The Hague had spread out and had seized the Deyl and the Haagsche Schouw, in this way controlling the approaches to The Hague. Meanwhile the Dutch troops in South Holland immediately began a counter-attack.

The remaining portion of the Third Battalion, Fourth Infantry Brigade, proceeded to attack the airfield of Valkenburg, which airfield was also attacked from the northwest and the northeast by the first and the second battalions of the same brigade. The Third Brigade, Second Artillery Regiment, gave the necessary artillery support in these attacks. Katwijk on the Rhine, where the Germans had meantime also gained a footing, was recovered by Second Battalion, Fourth Infantry Brigade. On the 10th May at 5.30 pm the airfield was again in Dutch hands. The German garrison retreated to the village of Valkenburg, where it maintained its position. The Third Brigade, Second Artillery Regiment, subjected this village to heavy artillery fire.

The Haagsche Schouw and the Deyl were re-conquered by young depot troops, the First Motor Cyclist Hussar Regiment also taking part in this operation. The German troops at these points also retreated to the village of Valkenburg.

First Battalion, Brigade of Grenadiers, which was on the southern outskirts of The Hague, received orders to re-conquer the airfield of Ockenburg by an attack from the north. This battalion, strengthened by depot troops, succeeded in retaking the airfield at 1.30 pm. The attack, thanks to the excellent short-wave communications, was effectively supported by the fire of First Brigade, Second Artillery Regiment, which had taken up its position near its permanent station at Poeldijk. The First Battalion, Brigade of Chasseurs, which was to attack the airfield from the direction of Monster, encountered resistance, in the course of its advance, near the estate of Ockenburg. When the battalion had wiped out this resistance at 4 pm the airfield was already in Dutch hands. The German garrison had retreated in a southwesterly direction.

Meantime, the airfield of Ypenburg had also been recovered by the Second and the Third Battalion, Brigade of Grenadiers, and young depot troops from The Hague.

In the latter city itself the fifth column had also displayed brisk activity. As early as the night of the 10th May men of the depot troops had installed a powerful guard service in the interior of the town. All action on the part of traitors was energetically countered and there were several instances of exchange of fire with fifth columnists inside houses.

View from the west to the east bank of the Meuse, taken at Casemate 66 S. in a practically northerly direction: (a) Church of Heyen; (b) Built road Afferden-Heyen; (c, d) The wooded land just opposite Casemate 67 S., from which attempts to cross were made.

The Meuse near Gennep and Grubbenvorst. The field of fire of Casemate 139 G.: (a) Church of Grubbenvorst; (b) Grubbenhoeve; (c) Grubbenvorst ferry station.

Under the threat of the German paratroops who had landed outside The Hague, the depot troops stationed at that place had occupied a position of defence on the north and east borders of that city. The enemy, however, did not carry out an attack on the city itself.

The Dutch troops in the Polder of the Hoeksche Waard and around Dordrecht took up defensive positions in order to prevent any extension of the success of the paratroops landed. In themselves, however, these units were not strong

COURSE OF MILITARY EVENTS ON THE 10TH MAY   35

Destroyed bridges over the Meuse, near Maastricht.

enough to undertake a counter-attack. The batteries of artillery at Strijen, armed with the out-of-date guns of 15 cm 24 length, directed fire during the whole of the day against Willemsdorp, the Moerdijk bridges and the Brabant shore. Unfortunately, the bridges were so strongly built that even continuous fire with high-explosive shells was not sufficient to render them unsuitable for traffic.

In the afternoon, the enemy landed reinforcements from aircraft on the shore south of Katwijk. These troops were fired on effectively from the sea by the Dutch naval vessel *Van Galen*, and they were also subjected to attacks by the Dutch air force. Finally, these troops were destroyed by units of the First Army Corps and depot troops.

An attack by German air-borne troops on the Staff Headquarters of The Hague group of the west front of the Holland Fortress at Wateringen was also beaten off with the aid of depot troops.

The Dutch air forces had meantime sustained heavy losses. What remained was concentrated on airfields concealed from the enemy. From there they were repeatedly sent out to attack, from the air, an enemy who continued to grow in overwhelming strength.

2. The Struggle in the Southern Provinces.

After the Dutch had carried out the work of destruction east of the Meuse (which was done before midnight of the 9th-10th May), the German troops passed over the Dutch frontier on a broad front in the early morning of the 10th May.

The main forces were directed on to the frontier section Lottum-Eysden, where subsidiary troops were sent forward against the part of the Meuse lying between Vierlingsbeek and Mook and the Meuse-Waal Canal.

The weak frontier guards east of the Meuse were speedily overpowered, after they had performed their duty of reporting the passages over the frontier.

Apart from the railway bridge at Gennep, all bridges over the Meuse were destroyed in time. The troops holding the bridge at Gennep, who were surprised by a German shock force, did not succeed in destroying the bridge. Because of this the structure lying in the second line, the railway viaduct at Beugen, the destruction of which had also been prepared, likewise fell undamaged into German hands. The consequence was that as early as 4 o'clock on the morning of the 10th May a German armoured train, followed by a train filled with infantry, passed over the Gennep bridge and the viaduct and steamed on to the railway halt called Zeeland in the rear of the Raam Peel position.

As early as 4 am German infantry appeared on the east bank of the portion of the Meuse between Sambeek, Boxmeer and Gennep, while the Dutch casemates on the west bank were speedily subjected to machine-gun and artillery fire. As the Dutch had no artillery at their disposal on the Meuse, the Dutch positions were defenceless against this artillery fire.

Between 5 and 9 o'clock am the attacker made five attempts to reach the west bank on the Mook-Gennep section with infantry, but all these attempts were repulsed by the well-directed machine-gun fire from the casemates occupied by troops of the Fifteenth Frontier Battalion and Second Battalion Twenty-Sixth Infantry Brigade.

Between 9 and 9.30 am the attackers succeeded in reaching the west bank in the neighbourhood of Gennep. The same was the case at Sambeek at about 10 am and at Mook at about 12 noon. After this the enemy was able to roll up the Dutch cordon position. At about 3 pm, therefore, the troops posted farther south on the Meuse were withdrawn to the Raam-Peel position.

At Venlo the German attack had been directed against the positions of the Third Battalion, Twenty-Sixth Brigade of Infantry, and the Second Frontier Battalion. From 4 to 9 am the enemy attempted to cross the Meuse in the vicinity of the blown-up bridge, and similar endeavours were made on that part of the Meuse lying south of Venlo and north of Kessel. At 9.15 am, under the protection of a smoke screen, the enemy succeeded in putting over a pontoon bridge south of Venlo, after which the Dutch position was rolled up there too. Some casemates, however, continued to offer resistance right into the morning of the 11th May.

After Grubbenvorst and Lottum had been subjected to artillery fire a passage of the river was also successfully effected at Lottum, which meant that the Dutch positions at Broekhuizen could also be taken in the rear. In this section, likewise, the troops remaining were ordered at 10.30 am to fall back on the Raam-Peel position.

In South Limburg, the first German tank division in action there had been able, by means of its artillery, to clear up the isolated casemates on the approach roads in a relatively short time, after which it pushed on towards Maastricht.

The orders of this division were:

(a) To gain mastery of the bridges at Maastricht, and

(b) After that, with the help of paratroops, to gain possession of the bridges, west of Maastricht, over the Belgian Albert Canal.

The bridges at Maastricht were, however, destroyed, so that the armoured division was only able to pass over to the other bank during the night of the 10th-11th May, after constructing a heavy pontoon bridge. The infantry troops had already got across.

On the Meuse-Waal Canal the bridge at Hatert was only partly blown up, so that the enemy was able to make his way over to the western bank into the positions of the First Battalion, Twenty-Sixth Brigade of Infantry, and to roll up the position on the west bank. On the afternoon of the 10th May the Dutch troops stationed there began their retreat to Tiel.

In this way, notwithstanding the heroic defence and self-sacrifice of the various troops occupying the casemates, the river line on the section Maastricht-Nijmegen had been broken through at several points by about 12 o'clock, and the enemy was able to continue his advance to the west.

Meantime troops belonging to the forces occupying the Raam-Peel position had also come into action.

The sector lying between the railway line Gennep-Uden and the Meuse, having a width of 10 km, was defended by three battalions belonging respectively to the Third, the Sixth and the Fourteenth Infantry Brigade. The troops were not equipped with up-to-date anti-tank guns, nor had they any mortars, or any means of defence against attack from the air. The only artillery support available was one brigade armed with guns of 8 cm steel (out-of-date guns without carriage brake and without gun-shields).

The German armoured train with the goods train following, which, owing to the negligence at the bridge of Gennep, had been able to drive through as far as the railway halt Zeeland, in the rear of the Raam-Peel position, landed German infantry units there, who immediately began an attack on the rear of the casemates lying north of the railway line and the casemates situated between the railway line and the metalled road Volkel-St. Huber.

Local reserves were not available. The artillery brigade Third Brigade, Twentieth Artillery Regiment, turned its guns round 180 degrees, however, and was in this way able to repel the attack on the casemates north of the railway. It was, however, not possible to prevent a number of casemates lying between the railway and the metalled road from falling into German hands at 7.30 am.

As a result of these events the commander of the Third Army Corps, who also had command of the light division, placed the Second Regiment of Motor Cyclist Hussars at the disposal of the territorial commander in North Brabant, with the object of recapturing the part of the position that had been lost.

The armoured train, which had meantime gone back, was derailed on the return journey owing to obstacles placed upon the line. A fight lasting hours developed between the occupants of this train and the casemates near the railway.

The counter-attack of the Second Motor Cyclist Hussars Regiment begun in the open area between the railway and the Volkel-St. Huber road was brought to a standstill by enemy machine-gun fire, and therefore did not attain the successful result which had been hoped for.

Meanwhile the German troops who had crossed the Sarnbeek-Mook portion of the Meuse had reached Mill, and at noon an attack developed from the environs of this place on the front of the position. The attack however, was repulsed by the First Battalion, Third Brigade of Infantry, which battalion occupied this part of the position.

Between 4 and 6 pm the German artillery then began violent fire on the Dutch section west of Mill, and this fire was between 6 and 7 pm followed by bombing by German aircraft. The village of Escharen lying farther north was also bombed and set on fire.

Having regard to the fact that the part of the section of the First Battalion, Third Brigade of Infantry, south of the railway line was in German hands, and that the counter-attack by the Second Motor Cyclist Hussar Regiment had not produced the desired result, while no reserves were available to carry out a fresh counter-attack, the whole of the troops occupying the Raam-Peel position were ordered to withdraw to the Zuid Willemsvaart during the night of the 10th-11th May. A screening force which stayed behind in the position till 4 am on the 11th May concealed this operation from the Germans, who therefore did not press on during the night.

Apart from certain troops who had not received the order of retreat, all the units had, in the early morning of the 11th May, taken up the positions ordered behind the Zuid Willemsvaart.

Meantime, as had been decided earlier, the Third Army Corps had moved from the encampment area south of 's Hertogenbosch to the front allocated to this unit behind the Waal between Ochten and Gorinchem.

The retreat was effected over the existing great connecting road between 's Hertogenbosch and Zalt Bommel, and by way of a second road farther east, the necessary pontoon bridges being constructed over the big rivers for this purpose.

Although the retreat had to be carried out by day and for the most part over entirely open terrain, the operation took place without enemy air attack.

The retreat of the Light Division was not so simple an affair.

This unit, too, had received orders in sealed envelopes for the retreat, which was to take place on the first night following an attack, if any. As in the case of the Third Army Corps, however, the Commander-in-Chief decided that the retreat was to start at once on the morning of the 10th May.

The two regiments of motorcyclist hussars had been withdrawn from the division. The First Regiment of Motorcyclist Hussars had already been placed at the disposal of the commander of the Holland Fortress even before the outbreak of hostilities. This was done in view of the danger from the air in the heart of the country. The second regiment was, as described above, placed under the orders of

COURSE OF MILITARY EVENTS ON THE 10TH MAY

the territorial commander in North Brabant on the morning of the 10th May. The Light Division now consisted, apart from the trains, of the two regiments of cyclists and the motorized corps of horse artillery.

According to orders prepared beforehand, the retreat was to take place:

(a) With the motorized section along the line of march Moerdijk, Dordrecht, Rotterdam, to the encampment point north of this place.

(b) With the First Cyclist Brigade along the axis Drongelen-Brakel-Herwijnen.

(c) With the Second Cyclist Brigade along the axis Keizersveer-Gorinchem.

As there was no bridge at this point, this brigade was to be transferred by ferry to the other bank.

In the early morning the staff of the Light Division received the news that the Moerdijk bridges were in German hands.

Orders were now modified, so that the motorized section, with the exception of the Horse Artillery Corps, was to follow the line of march of the Second Cyclist Brigade, while the Horse Artillery Corps was at first to do the same, but after passing over the bridge at Keizersveer, was to diverge to the marching route of the First Cyclist Brigade.

The Light Division was thus confronted with the difficult task of carrying out a march by day over roads for the most part narrow and open, with units having different marching paces. This, too, in a conflict with an opponent possessing air supremacy, while the anti-aircraft defence consisted only of a few obsolete batteries, set up at the bridges Keizersveer, Drongelen, and Brakel-Herwijnen, and a few platoons of anti-aircraft machine guns. The ferry at Sleeuwijk, indeed, had no protection whatever in the form of anti-aircraft defences.

Notwithstanding the fact that occasional hold-ups occurred, owing to the above circumstances, and that the columns were exposed to the attack of German aircraft, few losses were sustained.

At 10 am the commander of the light division received orders from the commander of the Third Army Corps to place himself, with the troops under his command, at the orders of the commander of the Holland Fortress, to be used, if necessary, for the occupation of the Merwede front lying between Dordrecht and Gorinchem. A brigade of cyclists was to proceed as quickly as possible to Gorinchem.

The commander of the light division thereupon gave orders for the occupation of the Merwede section by the two brigades of cyclists attacking side by side.

In the evening, however, the said commander received fresh orders from the commander of the Holland Fortress. These were to the following effect:

(a) To advance in the direction of Ysselmonde and attack the German troops which had landed at Waalhaven. The airfield in question was to be bombed by the RAF during the night of the 10th-11th May, but this bombing would have ended by 2.20 am.

(b) To place one battalion at the disposal of the cantonment commander at Dordrecht.

At 5.45 pm the commander of the Light Division issued fresh orders in this connection, whereby the division was to proceed to the Noord in two marching groups in order to cross this river at Alblasserdam.

On the River Noord itself the commander of the Light Division did not expect any resistance.

For the attack against Waalhaven the commander of the Light Division still disposed of five battalions of cyclists and two brigades of artillery (four batteries, sixteen guns in all). The battalion of cyclists intended for Dordrecht was, after crossing the bridge at Alblasserdam, to diverge towards Zwijndrecht.

The brigades of cyclists were meantime engaged in occupying the Merwede front, and therefore it was some time before the troops could begin the movement in execution of the new order. Not till 10.30 pm did the Second Cyclist Brigade start the movement from Sliedrecht, while the First Cyclist Brigade was at that moment marching forward near Laag Blokland.

Meantime it had become evident to the commander of the Light Division that the west bank of the Noord at Alblasserdam was occupied by the enemy and that the bridge had been swung open.

The battalion of cyclists intended for Dordrecht was therefore ordered to attain its objective by way of Papendrecht. In view of the lateness of the hour, the commander of the Light Division decided to postpone the attack on the German troops on the west bank of the Noord at Alblasserdam till the morning of the 11th May.

3. The Events in the Valley Positions, in the Area East of the Latter, and in the Northern Provinces.

In accordance with the orders given, the troops east of the Yssel carried out the destructions and set up the obstructions which had been prepared. The only case in which destruction was not successful was that of the bridge over the Twente Canal at Diepenheim. In accordance with their instructions the troops operating to the east of the Yssel withdrew thereafter behind the latter waterway.

All the bridges over the Yssel were then blown up.

In the early morning of the 10th May the German forces, operating chiefly along the axis Emmerik-Zevenaar-Arnhem, had already crossed the frontier. The frontier there being only a few kilometres away from the Yssel, this river was already reached by the Germans early in the morning. Supported by overwhelming artillery strength, the Germans succeeded at 10 am in crossing the Yssel at Westervoort and continuing their march along the axes Arnhem-Ede and Arnhem-Wageningen.

Meanwhile the troops in the Valley position had fully occupied their lines at 3 am on the 10th May. All the preparations for a prolonged defence had been made. The artillery units had made their preparations for firing at all the important points in the terrain facing them, from their normal position and two reserve positions. Only the floodwater in some depressions was lower than during the preceding period, probably in consequence of weather conditions.

COURSE OF MILITARY EVENTS ON THE 10TH MAY 41

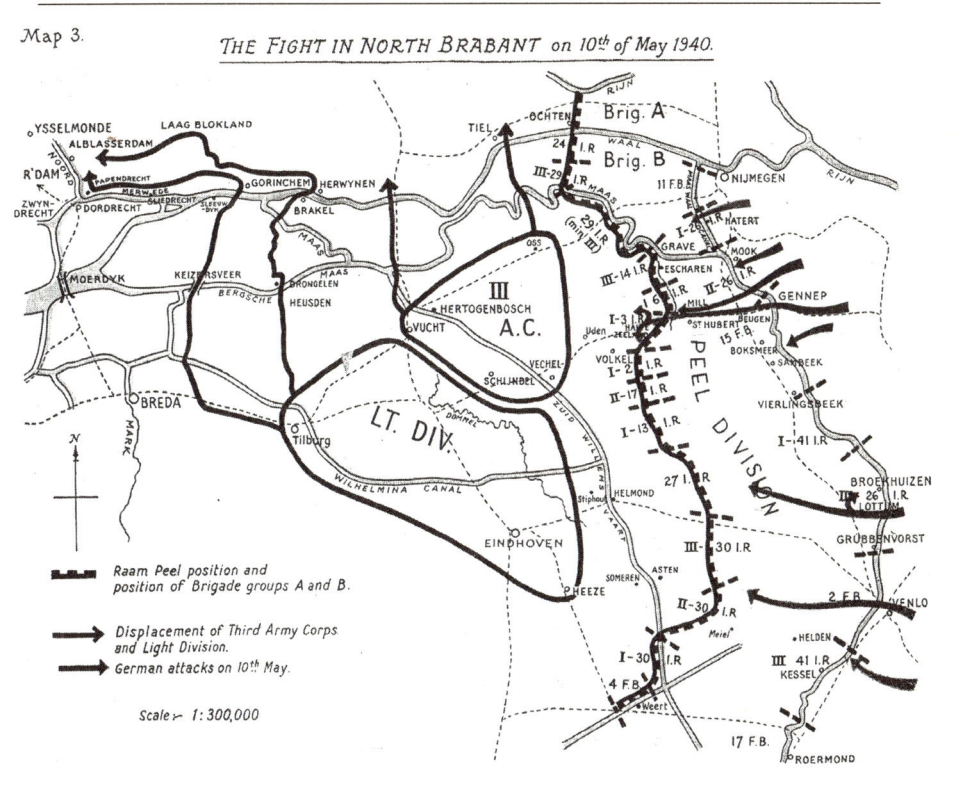

Map No. 3: The Fighting in North Brabant on the 10th May, 1940

The light troops belonging to the two army corps which occupied the Valley position were pushed forward – namely, First and Fifth Hussar Regiments in the section of the Fourth Army Corps and Fourth Hussar Regiment in the section of the Second Army Corps.

The task of the light troops in question was:

(a) To delay an enemy advance in the area west of the Yssel.

(b) To co-operate in, and to cover the execution of, the plan of destruction which had been prepared for this area.

As the field army fighting in the Valley position did not possess large reserves, the commander of the field army was very anxious, if possible, to get these regiments back intact inside the position area, and for this reason particular emphasis in the order was laid on its second part.

The delaying action by the said regiments was to begin in the line the Yssel from Arnhem to Spankeren, and afterwards along the Dieren Canal. The main bodies were to effect delay along the line Oosterbeek-Harskamp-Garderen-Ermelo-Harderwijk.

When the troops on the canal had carried out the work of destruction on the morning of the 10th May, they fell back on the main body.

The German troops who had broken through and passed over the Yssel at Westervoort soon came into contact with the Fourth Hussar Regiment, which regiment fought successive delaying actions at Oosterbeek, Heelsum, Renkum and Ede, finally retreating on the evening of the 16th May before the overwhelming strength of the Germans, behind the Valley position, and rallying at Leersum.

In consequence of the forced retreat of the Fourth Hussar Regiment the right wings of the First and Fifth Hussar Regiments were exposed, so that these regiments were drawn back to the line Groote Hoef - Klaarwater - Nijkerkerveen-Nijkerk.

Meantime, the events in the heart of Holland had prompted the Commander-in-Chief to withdraw six battalions of the field army from the defence of the Valley position. The large units in the front line were in this way deprived to a great extent of their reserves, so that the commander of the field army considered it necessary also to draw back the mounted squadrons of the First and Fifth Hussar Regiments behind the position, in order to form new reserves from these after their conversion into cyclist units. On the evening of the 10th May, therefore, all that remained on the terrain in front of the Valley position was the unmounted part of the First Hussar Regiment, which was in the line Klaarwater-Nijkerk.

While these events were in progress, the cordon disposition of the Dutch troops in the northern provinces had also been broken through by the German troops operating there. The port installations and the locks at Delfzijl were destroyed, and the entrance to the harbour was blocked, with a view to depriving the Germans of the use of the harbour as long as possible.

In the evening the troops which had operated in the northern provinces passed through the Wons position at the head of the outer Zuider Zee dyke. From there they were transported to Den Helder, where they were reorganized in order to continue the fight.

4. *The Situation at the End of the First Day of War.*

Therefore the position at the end of the first day of war was as follows:

(a) The troops operating east of the great rivers, after carrying out the task allotted to them – namely, safeguarding the destruction which had been prepared in these regions – had either retreated or been destroyed.

(b) The waterline formed by the rivers Meuse and Yssel, with the Meuse-Waal Canal lying between, and the line of canals in the northern provinces had been broken through, after they had, however, delayed the German advance for four to six hours.

Apart from one single structure, all the bridges on the waterline were destroyed, with the result that the German armies operating to the west of the rivers experienced great difficulties in their supplies and rear communications.

A part of the troops occupying the line of the rivers had been able to withdraw into the Valley position or the Raam-Peel position.

COURSE OF MILITARY EVENTS ON THE 10TH MAY

(c) The light troops east of the Valley position had been withdrawn into that position except for a small number on the northern front. The enemy, however, had not yet made contact with the advance posts.

(d) The Raam-Peel position had been broken through south of Mill, and the troops occupying this position were to withdraw to the Zuid Willemsvaart on the night of the 10th-11th May.

(e) The German attack on the heart of the country, the object of which was to gain possession on the very first day of the centre of government, The Hague, had been repulsed, and all the airfields around The Hague had been recovered. The small bodies of paratroops which were still north of the Meuse no longer presented any real danger. Clearing them up was only a question of time.

Rotterdam, however, in so far as it lay south of the Meuse, with the airfield of Waalhaven, had not been recovered. The entire island of Ysselmonde, and the greater portion of the island of Dordrecht, with the two Moerdijk bridges, were in German hands.

In addition, the entire First Army Corps was engaged with this enemy and was therefore diverted from its proper task, that of forming the reserve for the field army in the Valley position, and, in case of need, re-occupation of the eastern front of the Holland Fortress. In addition, six battalions of the reserve of the great units in the Valley position had been taken away from these units and despatched to the Holland Fortress.

(f) The Third Army Corps and the Light Division had carried out the retreat indicated above under difficult circumstances practically without loss. The said army corps had taken up its positions on the Waal, while the Light Division had marched forward for the attack on the Waalhaven airfield.

Chapter Nine

The Military Operations on the 11th May

1. The Fighting in the Heart of the Country and on the Southern Front of the Holland Fortress.

On this day, too, the fifth column operating at The Hague proved very active. The troops composing the first division were engaged for the most part in destroying the last centres of resistance occupied by paratroops in the environs of The Hague.

The First Battalion of the Brigade of Chasseurs for this purpose carried out engagements at Belvedere in the neighbour-hood of Ockenburg, while the Fourth Brigade of Infantry, which was later on reinforced by the Ninth Brigade of Infantry of the third division, was fighting for the possession of the village of Valkenburg. The remaining troops continued to occupy the recovered airfields.

At Rotterdam and Ysselmonde the German forces had, however, meantime been continually reinforced.

True, the airfield at Waalhaven had been made useless as such by the artillery fire directed on it, but in its place the parking space of Feyenoord was used by the German aircraft in order to land reinforcements.

As regards means of access to the southern front of the Holland Fortress, the bridge at Heusden had meantime been blown up. The bridge at Keizersveer was in Dutch hands, but was exposed to German air attack during the course of the 11th May, while the Moerdijk bridges were still in German hands.

Meanwhile mechanized parts of the seventh French Army, after marching through Belgium, had reached North Brabant on the 11th May.

Request was made by the Dutch to the French Supreme Command to push on as rapidly as possible with these forces in order to attack the Moerdijk bridges from the southern side.

The expectation that German resistance on the island of Dordrecht and Ysselmonde would be broken by the action of the French forces in question, and also by the attack of the light division on the 11th May, was, however, not fulfilled. It is true that a French mechanized squadron made its appearance on the southern bank of the Hollandsch Diep opposite Strijen, but attacks by German bombers compelled these troops to withdraw. The attack of the Light Division over the Noord also made no progress.

According to the order of attack of the commander of the light division issued during the evening of the 10th May, at 11 o'clock, the two brigades of cyclists were to cross the Noord on the morning of the 11th May, north and south of Alblasserdam respectively.

As one battalion of cyclists had been sent to Dordrecht and another was to form the divisional reserve, four battalions were available for attack.

MILITARY OPERATIONS ON THE 11TH MAY

The defence canal in front of the Peel position, with one of the casemates in the foreground.

When day dawned, the Second Brigade of Cyclists succeeded in getting over a few patrols by surprise. They were, however, unable to maintain themselves in the area occupied by the enemy.

An attempt made later with bigger forces, 1 km south of Alblasserdam, was successful to the extent that a first echelon of sixty men reached the west bank. The enemy having meantime received reinforcements, however, these troops were unable to follow up the success they had secured, and it was likewise impossible to reinforce the echelon which had crossed.

An attempt at crossing north of Alblasserdam was nipped in the bud by murderous fire of enemy machine guns. No artillery support could, as yet, be given on our side, because the Corps of Horse Artillery had not yet been able to take up any position.

Therefore, on the morning of the 11th May, four battalions of cyclists lay extended along the eastern bank of the Noord. At 10.10 am heavy German air attacks were made on these forces. In these circumstances the commander of the Light Division felt that it was impossible for him, with the means at his disposal, to carry out the order to advance to Waalhaven.

The commander of the Holland Fortress, having been informed of this view, changed his order to the following:

> (a) A part of the Light Division was to clear the island of Dordrecht of the enemy and afterwards to endeavour to move on to Waalhaven by way of Wieldrecht, the ferry of s' Gravendeel, and Barendrecht.

> (b) The rest of the Light Division were to hold the east bank of the Noord.

In addition, another battalion of cyclists was to be placed as speedily as possible at the disposal of the cantonment commander of Dordrecht.

The execution of this last order was allocated to the First Battalion of the Second Brigade of Cyclists, which was on the farthest southern wing of the position on the Noord.

46   MILITARY OPERATIONS OF THE DUTCH ARMY

Meuse Waal Canal at Neerbosch. The bridge on the great main road Nijmegen-Grave is still destroyed. The railway bridge alongside is once more in use for a single track. In addition the bridge to the north at Neerbosch is restored. The battle positions of the Netherlands troops are still visible on the west bank. Photograph taken in July 1941; scale about 1:14,000.

Meantime, the units in the foremost line were again subjected to violent air bombing at 12.40, 12.50, 2 and 2.15 pm. The Second Battalion of the Second Brigade of Cyclists were in this way broken up and retreated to the east after the First Battalion of the Second Brigade of Cyclists had marched off at 2 pm to Papendrecht, and therefore there were only two battalions of cyclists left on the east bank of the Noord.

Meantime, the Light Division had been reinforced by the Second Motor Cyclist Hussar Regiment, which, having suffered very heavy losses in the fighting at

Bridges over the Waal at Nijmegen. The bridge on the great main road Nijmegen-Arnhem is still destroyed. The railway bridge is again in use for a single track. Photograph taken in July 1941; scale about 1:11,000.

Mill on the 10th May, had returned once more to the division, while the commander of the Third Army Corps also placed the First Brigade of the Eleventh Regiment of Artillery (armed with 10 cm medium artillery) at the disposal of the Divisional Commander.

The new orders which were issued by the commander of the Light Division directed that:

> (a) A holding group on the Noord should be formed by the First Cyclist Brigade, minus the Second Battalion and First Brigade of the Horse Artillery Corps.

(b) The principal group, which was to mop up the enemy in the island of Dordrecht, and afterwards to push on to Waalhaven, would consist of the Second Brigade of Cyclists, the Second Battalion of the First Brigade of Cyclists, and the Second Brigade of the Horse Artillery Corps.

The battalions of cyclists already sent to Dordrecht could therefore be included in this group.

Finally, the divisional reserve could be formed by the machine-gun squadron belonging to the division and Second Motor Cyclist Hussar Regiment.

The air forces on that day bombed the German forces south of the Moerdijk. At the same time they brought in reports of the presence of several hundred paratroops, who were stated to be south and southeast of Dordrecht.

The remainder of the fighter aircraft squadrons, which had fought so bravely, were grouped together. All together these units were left with no more than twelve damaged machines.

2. *The Military Operations in North Brabant.*

After a night march during the night of the 10th-11th May, the troops occupying the Raam-Peel position, reinforced by some units, which had remained intact, of the troops which originally held the Meuse, reached the Zuid Willemsvaart on the early morning of the 11th May, and occupied the west bank of this canal.

The retreat took place without interference by the enemy, who, probably misled by the screening force left behind in the position till 4 am, did not discover until the morning of the 11th May that the Raam-Peel position had been abandoned by the Dutch troops.

In order to cover the retreat the First Battalion of the Forty-First Brigade of Infantry had also taken up a position on the eastern border of Helmond.

Notwithstanding the fact that the troops had been in actual operations uninterruptedly for nearly thirty-six hours, they immediately set to work to put the west bank into a state of defence, and proceeded to destroy the bridges over the canal.

As was already pointed out when dealing with Dutch geography from the military point of view, the Zuid Willemsvaart is unfavourable as a position. Not only do the dykes restrict the field of fire extremely and make it necessary to arrange the guns in a straight line, without depth, but in addition to this there are extensive built-up areas on the east bank.

A strength of about twelve battalions was still available to hold this position. Here, just as in the Raam-Peel position, anti-aircraft defence and anti-tank defence were entirely lacking, and again, as regards artillery, only a few batteries of 8 cm (steel) were available. If, in addition, it is taken into consideration that the length of the section to be defended was about 70 km, no great hopes could be entertained as regards the length of time the resistance might last.

On the morning of the 11th May the Germans drew near chiefly along the axes:
Grave-'s Hertogenbosch;
Mill-Uden-Vechel;
Venlo-Helden-Meyel-Asten; and
Roermond-Weert.

At 11 am German patrols appeared on the east bank.

MILITARY OPERATIONS ON THE 11TH MAY

Little by little the pressure increased, especially in that part of the position which lay between Someren and Stiphout.

The Dutch troops tried to prevent passage of the canal with all the weapons at their disposal. Several armoured cars were disabled by the 6 cm light artillery.

The attackers, taking advantage of the very much greater strength of artillery which they possessed, the fire of which they directed particularly to those parts of the canal where there were conglomerations of tall buildings, were able shortly after noon to reach the west bank at several points, among others at Someren and south of Vechel, whereupon they began to roll up the Dutch position.

In these circumstances a retreat was again ordered, with a view to falling back successively on the lines formed by the Dommel and the Wilhelmina Canal.

Meantime, conditions had become very unfavourable for the Dutch forces fighting here.

The supply trains of several sections of the forces had fallen into German hands. Other units, which reached the Zuid Willemsvaart at the moment when the bridges over this canal had already been blown up, had thrown their vehicles into the canal in order to prevent them falling into the hands of the enemy. Finally, columns of vehicles belonging to the various units had been broken up by the persistent German air attacks.

When it was found in the course of the retreat that the bridges over the Wilhelmina Canal had already been blown up, while in addition there was no longer any sense in taking up a position behind this canal, because the Germans – having crossed the Zuid Willemsvaart near Vechel – were already in the rear of the proposed new position, the orders were altered, and the line Tilburg-Breda-Roosendaal was laid down as the general line of retreat.

The main roads were exposed to continuous attacks by German aircraft, and were littered with burned and destroyed vehicles. The troops in question, therefore, endeavoured as best they could to reach the western part of North Brabant by moving in small numbers along the inner roads.

Motorized parts of the seventh French Army, which had reached the line Tilburg-Best in the course of the afternoon, also fell back to the west on Breda.

In this way, on the evening of the 11th May, the way to Zeeland and the south front of the Holland Fortress lay practically open to the attacker.

3. Events in the Valley Position and in the Northern Provinces.

German troops had already made their appearance before Renkum on the evening of the 10th May, and on the 11th May an attack was made on the advance posts of the most southerly regimental section of the fourth division. The position of the Third Battalion of the First Brigade of Infantry, which occupied this advance post area, was then pierced. Farther to the north the advance posts were exposed to slight pressure only. The attacker, having forced in the advance posts in the section of the Eighth Brigade of Infantry, shifted his artillery fire forward, in consequence of which the principal area of resistance in the section held by the Eighth Brigade of Infantry, in particular close to the Grebbeberg, was exposed to heavy artillery fire during the whole of the afternoon and evening. Enemy infantry pushing along the broad approach at Wageningen, were able in the evening to make fighting contact in this part of the position with the troops in the principal area of resistance.

50   MILITARY OPERATIONS OF THE DUTCH ARMY

Bridge over the Noord at Alblasserdam. On 11th May the Light Division tried in vain to cross this waterline north and south of the bridge. Photograph taken July 1943; scale about 1:20,000.

Rhenen, lying farther to the rear, was also subjected to enemy artillery fire, while our own artillery directed its fire to Scherpenzeel, Wageningen and the metalled road Ede-Renswoude.

Meantime, the enemy opposite the front of the Fourth Army Corps showed not the slightest activity. The First Regiment of Hussars, which was still in front of the advance posts, passed behind these positions owing to a mistake. In the evening, however, the regiment resumed its original position.

One point of weakness for the defence of the Valley position, however, was that the Supreme Command of the land and sea forces, under the pressure of events in the interior of the country, found it necessary to withdraw all armoured cars from the field army, with the exception of one section. Coming in addition to the withdrawal of the infantry battalions from this army, which had already taken place, this meant a further weakening of the Valley army.

Notwithstanding the enemy air supremacy, reconnaissance aircraft carried out their work successfully over the Yssel and the Veluwe.

In the northern provinces the German Forces had meanwhile reached Harlingen and Franeker, while on the night of the 11th-12th May Stavoren was occupied. After the breakthrough on the canal front, the attacker had here met with practically no further resistance.

In the evening enemy reconnaissance detachments also appeared before the Wons position, and fighting contact was made with that position.

4. *The Military Position at the End of the Second Day of War.*

Therefore, at the end of the second day of war, the position on the east front gave no ground for anxiety.

Though the advance posts on the southern part of the Valley position had been forced in, and contact had been made there with the main position, the occupation of this area was still intact over the entire length and depth of the position.

There still remained the difficulty that no large reserves were available in the Valley position. Not only were the reserves which had been previously diverted for the defence of the heart of the country still in operation there, and not only was the First Army Corps fully engaged with the fighting in the province of South Holland, but even on the second day of war forces were withdrawn from the Valley army for the defence of the interior of the country.

Even the loss of the northern provinces, however regrettable, was no final obstacle to the further conduct of the defence. The approaches to Holland, running over the separating dyke, were still firmly in Dutch hands. The Wens position, and also the work in the second line behind it on the Kornwerderzand, were both still entirely intact.

The position in the south was more serious.

Attempts to drive the enemy from the island of Ysselmonde had failed at Rotterdam and at Alblasserdam, while the Moerdijk bridges and the major part of the island of Dordrecht were still in German hands. The forces of the enemy had even received considerable additions in the course of the 11th May. Furthermore, the resistance of the Dutch troops in North Brabant had collapsed. If the French forces did not succeed in retaking the Moerdijk bridges on the 12th May and checking the German advance in the outermost line Breda-Moerdijk, it was probable that the German troops operating in Brabant would make contact on the 12th May with the German air-borne infantry and paratroops around Dordrecht and at Ysselmonde.

An appeal for support addressed to our Allies could not be complied with by them because they were themselves fully occupied with the struggle taking place in Belgium and Northern France. Even from the British air force support could only be obtained locally and on a very modest scale.

In these circumstances all the forces in the province of South Holland were fully tied up there and the urgently necessary reinforcement of the troops occupying the Valley position could not take place on that day either.

Chapter Ten

Military Operations on the 12th May

(See Maps 1 and 4)

1. The Struggle in the Heart of the Country and on the Southern Front of the Holland Fortress.

On this day, too, light fighting actions took place around The Hague against paratroops and air-borne infantry, which were still holding out at a few points.

Near Leyden the Fourth Brigade of Infantry continued its attack on the village of Valkenburg from the direction of Katwijk, where the German infantrymen who had retreated from the airfield were still defending themselves.

In view of further possible German actions from the air, the First Army Corps still had to carry on now with the task of holding important points and airfields in the heart of Holland, and this army corps could not be employed for other fighting actions.

In the fight at Rotterdam, German artillery now intervened for the first time. The Dutch artillery in the Hoeksche Waard changed their position that they might direct their fire on to the southern embankment of Rotterdam and Waalhaven. The airfields of Waalhaven itself and Feyenoord were again attacked by the last remnants of the Dutch air force.

The Dutch artillery stationed on the southern border of the Hoeksche Waard – out-of-date 15 cm guns – put out their full strength of fire in order to prevent passage over the Moerdijk bridges. In this process they were, of course, continually exposed themselves to the fire of enemy artillery and attacks of German aircraft, considerable losses being sustained and heavy damage done to the guns. They did not succeed in preventing the crossing from Brabant to the island of Dordrecht, on the morning of the 12th May, of the advance portions of the German armoured division, which had made its way through North Brabant, and of units of the Waffen SS.

In the meantime the group of the Light Division which had received orders to clear the island of Dordrecht, and thereafter to advance towards Rotterdam, had been fighting, successfully at first, in the environs of Dordrecht against the German forces there, which were, moreover, continually strengthened by new landings of parachute troops and air-borne infantry. When, however, on the morning of the 12th May, the forces of the German tank division and the units of the Waffen SS were able to throw their weight into the scales, the battalions of cyclists were compelled to retire, and the German armoured troops were able, shortly after noon, to make contact with the air-borne troops fighting on the south embankment of Rotterdam.

In this way one of the decisive episodes of the campaign had been completed.

MILITARY OPERATIONS ON THE 12TH MAY

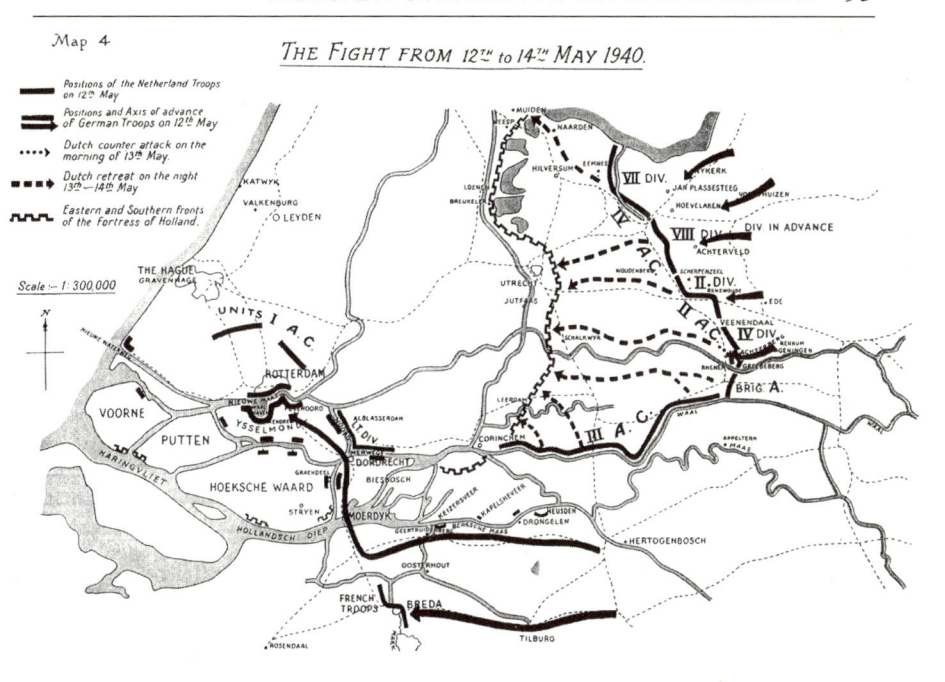

Map No. 4: The Fighting from the 12th to 14th May, 1940

The Dutch troops in the Hoeksche Waard and the holding group of the Light Division on the Noord maintained their defensive position, in order to prevent the German forces on the island of Dordrecht and on Ysselmonde from extending over the adjoining islands.

Above all, the troops of the Light Division on the Noord were in this case exposed to air bombing and artillery fire, which was answered as effectively as possible by the Dutch artillery.

East of the Moerdijk the points of passage over the Bergsche Maas at the bridge of Keizersveer, at the ferries of Kapelle and Drongelen, and at the bridge of Heusden were still in Dutch hands.

2. *The Military Operations in North Brabant.*

In North Brabant practically no further fighting of importance took place on this day.

The remnants of the Dutch troops who had been the original troops occupying the Meuse and the Raam-Peel position endeavoured in small bodies to escape the grip of the Germans. Since the night of the 9th-10th May, these troops had practically not had a moment of rest. For them these days of war had been a succession of taking up positions, fighting delaying actions, and long and wearisome marches in retreat, in which, owing to lack of anti-aircraft defence, they were exposed, practically defenceless, to the attacks of the German air forces.

Part of them succeeded in escaping by way of the bridge at Keizersveer to the Holland Fortress. Other bodies were able to reach the islands of Zeeland, where they were reorganized to continue the struggle.

Bridge over the Noord at Alblasserdam.

Some of them, by order of the officer in command of the French troops who had taken up positions near Breda, were sent on to Antwerp and then despatched to Zeeland Flanders.

A large number, including the staff of the Peel division, which met with this fate at Tilburg, fell into German hands as prisoners.

The French, who had originally planned to resist the German advance along the general line, the Mark as far as Breda, Oosterhout, Geertruidenberg, were compelled to withdraw their left wing under German pressure, thus throwing open to the Germans the way to Moerdijk.

For the present, however, they still maintained their plan of stubbornly defending Breda. Consequently, on the evening of the 12th May, they sent the entire population of that town, 40,000 persons, into Belgium.

3. *The Fighting in the Valley Position and in the Northern Provinces.*

On the morning of the 12th May the enemy artillery continued its fire against the main position in the section of the fourth division. The firing was particularly violent in the most southerly part, the environs of the Grebbeberg.

The artillery of the fourth division, supported by the army corps artillery and by a part of the contiguous division to the left, endeavoured to answer this fire as best they could, and to gain the upper hand over the attacking German artillery. In this, however, owing to the superior artillery strength of the enemy, they were not successful.

The attacks by the Dutch air force on the German artillery positions at Wageningen were also ineffective in destroying this artillery.

Under cover of its artillery and supported by the air force, the German attacking infantry was gradually able to penetrate as far as the Grebbeberg, and subsequently to extend the success secured by infiltration. The battalions of the Eighth Brigade of Infantry offered the fiercest resistance, sustaining heavy losses. Local counter-attacks gave relief for a time, but the troops engaged did not succeed in retaking the whole of the ground lost.

Therefore, when night fell the attackers had succeeded in penetrating as far as the last defence line, and the chief resistance in this section had been practically broken through.

MILITARY OPERATIONS ON THE 12TH MAY 55

The Grebbeberg, south flank of the Valley position. The old Netherlands fortifications – superseded, however, by modern casemates of reinforced concrete – can be seen clearly on the photograph. The extension of the Valley Position in the territory between the Rijn and the Waal, with the fortification of "De Spees" at its north flank, is also visible. On the bottom left-hand side of the photograph is the railway siding of Kesteren. Photograph taken August 1943; scale about 1:20,000.

Those troops of the Eighth Brigade of Infantry which had remained intact retired and took up a new position behind the railway line, Rhenen-Veenendaal, lying in a deep depression.

In the section of the second division, meanwhile, the advance posts and the troops on the principal strip of resistance were exposed to heavy artillery action, while there also the attacking infantry gradually gained ground. Consequently, the advance posts in this section of the division were also drawn back to the main ground of defence.

Opposite the section of the Fourth Army Corps the enemy on this day also showed no activity whatever.

In order to gain a view of what was happening in the enemy lines in front of this army corps, the army corps commander gave the First Regiment of Hussars, which was still in the line Hoevelaken-Jan Plassesteeg, the order to carry out reconnaissance towards the line Achterveld-Voorthuisen-Nijkerk.

The regimental commander thereupon sent out three reconnaissance detachments in the directions mentioned.

The Achterveld detachment encountered the main body of an advancing German division and was destroyed.

The Voorthuisen detachment likewise, at the last-mentioned village, came into contact with strong enemy forces, which partly destroyed the detachment, though a part of it escaped.

The Nijkerk detachment came into contact with the enemy at Nijkerk itself. As meantime enemy troops coming from the south had reached the line of retreat of this detachment, the whole of it was taken prisoner by the enemy.

Meanwhile, the reconnaissance by the First Regiment of Hussars had shown that opposite the front of the Fourth Army Corps heavy German forces were advancing and that their contact with the Fourth Army Corps could be expected at any moment.

In the northern provinces, meanwhile, the attack on the Wons position had begun.

The enemy had already made fighting contact with this position on the previous evening, and in the morning he opened heavy artillery fire against the Dutch, particularly against the northern and middle sections of the position. Violent air bombing strengthened the effect of this artillery fire. Deprived of all artillery support themselves and of anti-air defence, the small body of Dutch troops – a reinforced infantry battalion – was exposed practically defenceless to this hurricane of fire. The fighting positions consisted only of simple earthworks, while the water in the flooding in front of the position had not been raised to the right level.

Towards noon the enemy proceeded to attack in the north and middle sections, and the enemy troops succeeded in penetrating into the position. A counter-attack, launched with the feeble local reserves available, did not produce the result hoped for. When, in addition, German tank troops succeeded in making their way over the dry parts of the ground to the rear of the position, it became untenable and the troops began to retreat, some over the Zuider Zee dyke, while the men occupying the southern section were transported by boat over the Ysselmeer to Medemblik.

The enemy immediately continued his advance, and on the very same evening made contact with the works on the Kornwerderzand.. The German air force began bombing these works, but the effect of the action against the heavily concreted positions was slight.

On the Ysselmeer the guard flotilla was reinforced by British and French motor torpedo boats.

As there was a train ferry at Stavoren, which had not been taken away to Holland, the harbour was subjected to fire by the Dutch naval vessel Friso. This warship, however, was then sunk by German bombers.

In order to strengthen the naval forces on the Ysselmeer, the Dutch naval vessel Gruno was posted to the guard flotilla.

4. The Situation at the End of the Third Day of War.

On the third day of war the position had become considerably worse for the Dutch forces.

Not only had the French troops operating in North Brabant failed to check the German advance, but powerful German units had even reached the neighbourhood of Rotterdam. This meant that it was no longer to be expected that troops could be drawn from Holland particularly the First Army Corps – for the defence of the Valley position.

Matters were still more serious now that this position had been broken through, though only locally and over a narrow width, while again only a few reserves were available to close the breach and restore the original position.

The Fourth Army Corps was pinned down by the German forces reported to be advancing against them, the Third Army Corps extended to cover a section of the Waal, about 50 km in length.

In the northern provinces the Germans had advanced as far as the head of the Zuider Zee dyke. The works on the Kornwerderzand were, however, quite intact, while the occupying troops awaited the enemy attack in full confidence and courage. Therefore, this part of the front gave rise to no anxiety for the moment.

Chapter Eleven

The Events of the 13th and 14th May

(See Maps 1 and 4)

1. The Fighting in the Valley Position and the Retreat to the East Front of the Holland Fortress.

The fact that the Valley position had been broken through over a narrow front near Rhenen on the evening of the 12th May imposed upon the Dutch Army Command the necessity of attempting to regain the lost ground by a counter-attack, if they wished to continue the defence in the Valley position.

As was already stated above, the struggle in the heart of Holland had deprived the large units in the Valley position of their local reserves, and units of the First Army Corps were likewise not available.

The only troops at the disposal of the Valley army for such an action were the units of the independent Brigade Group B. The said brigade had originally been stationed in the land between the Waal and the Meuse, in order to form with the independent Brigade Group A the connecting link between the troops occupying the Valley position and those in the Raam-Peel position. When the Raam-Peel position was abandoned there was no longer any sense in the independent Brigade Group B remaining south of the Waal, and therefore this unit was withdrawn to the north of this river.

The brigade now had only a strength of four infantry battalions, while the brigade artillery was not more than a few batteries of out-of-date guns. Nevertheless, the forces available were got ready for an attack from the northwest against the enemy, who had penetrated the position.

When day broke on the 13th May the attack was started, after artillery preparation in which the artillery of the Second Army Corps also took part.

With Rhenen burning in the background the Dutch battalions endeavoured to work their way forward through the covered terrain.

At first the attack was successful, but finally it broke down at Achterberg under the overwhelming fire of the German artillery, violent bombing from the air, and the fire of the automatic weapons.

The failure of this heroic attempt forced upon the Dutch Army Command the difficult decision of ordering the whole of the troops occupying the Valley position to withdraw to the east front of the Holland Fortress. If this retreat had had to take place during the day, it would have meant the destruction of the Valley army, owing to the absolute air supremacy of the German air force and the narrow and largely open roads. Therefore, the Valley position had to be held in any case till the evening of the 13th May. Notwithstanding the intense enemy artillery fire and the aircraft racing overhead, the Dutch infantry were successful in preventing the German attackers from developing their success during the entire day.

EVENTS OF THE 13TH AND 14TH MAY 59

In the afternoon of the 13th May the warning order was given respecting a retreat which was to take place in a north-westerly direction, and the definitive orders for retreat followed later. The Valley troops began their retreat at 9 pm, leaving behind a screening force till the early morning of the 14th May.

The sectors of retreat indicated for the divisions were, in a general sense:

Seventh Division: Loenen-Muiden.

Eighth Division: Region northeast and east of Utrecht.

Second Division: Region southeast of Utrecht.

Fourth Division: Section between the Waal and Jutphaas.

The retreat was effected in the night under the most difficult circumstances. Although the flooding on the eastern front of the Holland Fortress had not been brought up to the full level, precisely with a view to the possibility of a retreat, the ground off the roads was in many places impassable, so that all the columns had to squeeze together on the few roads which passed through the flooded territory. Obviously, confusion and hold-ups were inevitable under these conditions.

Thanks to the screening troops left behind, the German troops remained entirely ignorant of the retreat which had been carried out. If tank units had pressed on along the roads during the night, the conditions would have been far more difficult still for the Dutch troops.

Nevertheless, on the morning of the 14th May the main body of the troops had reached the places where they were ordered to take up positions, and the utterly weary men were able to set about occupying the eastern front of the Holland Fortress.

One difficulty which arose in this connection was that, in considering the possibility of a retreat, it had been expected that the First Army Corps would occupy certain important parts of the terrain. But this corps was no longer available for the fighting on the east front, and therefore fresh provision had to be made in this respect also.

In spite of all these circumstances, the troops on the eastern front looked forward with confidence to further fighting on the morning of the 14th May.

The flood locks, now fully opened, made the water level rise visibly. The Germans, surprised by the retreat, required a pause before they could resume their advance, so that the first troops did not appear before the position until the afternoon.

The Dutch troops, however, were not given the opportunity of measuring their strength against the attacker on this historic ground.

2. *The Military Operations in North Brabant and at the Kornwerderzand.*

Under the pressure of the German advance the French were compelled as early as the 13th May to abandon the resistance offered on the line Turnhout-Breda, and they fell back on Roosendaal. At the request of the local French commander, portions of the Dutch troops from the Raam-Peel position, which were in the environs of Bergen op Zoom, took up a position south of this place in order to cover the French troops in the rear against a possible landing of parachute troops.

On the 14th May the French were also compelled to abandon the position at Roosendaal, and they fell back on the Antwerp Fortress, which at that time still formed the left wing support of the Allied troops in the Dyle position: Namur-Louvain-Antwerp.

Whatever Dutch troops still remained in West Brabant at that moment withdrew into Belgium in order from there to be transported to Zeeland Flanders for the continuation of the struggle.

In the northern provinces the Germans, after having made contact on the evening of the 12th May with the defence works at Kornwerderzand, had begun their attack on the last-mentioned fortifications.

The works in question were subjected to heavy air bombing again on the morning of the 13th May, and in the afternoon the German artillery also opened fire against the casemates. The works on the Kornwerderzand had no artillery forces of their own, and therefore the Dutch air force was ordered to attack the German artillery positions. Effective fire was also directed against this artillery by the Dutch naval vessel *Johan Maurits van Nassau*, which had steamed up for this purpose from Den Helder to the sea arm of Texel.

A German infantry attack over the dyke, launched in the afternoon, collapsed under the fire of the automatic guns from the casemates.

The morning of the 14th May started with a renewed heavy air bombing, which caused some damage to the casemates, but was in no wise successful in breaking down the power of resistance of the occupying troops.

3. *The Events in the Heart of the Country.*

In the heart of the country the condition on the 13th May underwent no material change. The German forces which had pressed on as far as the south bank of the Meuse at Rotterdam did not succeed in extending their success and reaching the north bank.

The Dutch forces were likewise not in a position to drive out the German troops from the islands of Ysselmonde and the island of Dordrecht. They had to confine themselves to preventing the Germans from deploying east and west by maintaining their positions on the east bank of the Noord and in the Hoeksche Waard.

If, as operations went on, the German troops were successful in reaching the north bank of the Meuse, their further advance to The Hague would be held up near Delft, for which purpose Dutch troops of the First Army Corps had taken up a position there. An enemy advance in the direction of Gouda would be checked in a similar way.

In order to be certain of retaining, in any case, the further conduct of the war against the aggressors, if the struggle should later on take an unexpected turn for the worse, the Dutch Government wisely decided to transfer itself to England. The further command of the defence was then entrusted with full confidence to the Commander of the Land and Sea Forces, General Winkelman, who had in the preceding days proved himself fully competent to carry out the very difficult task placed upon him.

In the morning of the 14th May again the state of affairs near Rotterdam underwent no change. All that happened was that in the Hoeksche Waard the Dutch troops were withdrawn to Strijen, and later to the west part of the island.

4. The Situation on the Morning of the 14th May, and the Capitulation.

If we look at the Holland Fortress into which the Dutch troops had withdrawn completely on the morning of the 14th May (apart from Zeeland, which was still intact in Dutch hands) the position was that:

> (a) German efforts to penetrate into the Fortress over the Zuider Zee dyke in the north had failed. The gateway giving access over this dyke – the works at the Kornwerderzand – were completely in the possession of the Dutch.
>
> (b) The east front of the Holland Fortress, from Muiden, by way of Utrecht, to Gorinchem, was entirely intact. The troops of the Valley army had taken up their positions on this front, and on the basis of the effect of the flooding the further course of the struggle could be looked forward to with confidence at this point.
>
> (c) The south front of the Holland Fortress had been broken through at the Moerdijk, and the enemy had succeeded in advancing in this section to the south bank of the Meuse at Rotterdam.

Nevertheless on this section there was still a continuous Dutch line of defence along the north bank of the Merwede, the east bank of the Noord, and the north bank of the Nieuwe Maas and the Nieuwe Waterweg. Furthermore, the islands of Voorne and Putten, and likewise the Hoeksche Waard, were still in Dutch hands, and the First Army Corps, strengthened by young depot troops, stood ready north of Rotterdam to check a further German advance in that direction.

Though the conditions of the defensive forces did not constitute any immediate ground for giving up the struggle, the position as regards defence against air attack was different.
The Dutch air force had been wiped out for all practical purposes, while the anti-aircraft artillery, weak in itself, began to suffer from shortage of ammunition. In these circumstances the German air force possessed practically complete supremacy in the air.
The German Army command did not fail to take every advantage, without the slightest scruple, of this decisive factor. Realizing that the German forces would, in the most favourable circumstances, require some days yet to break down the Dutch resistance, the German Army command had recourse to the most barbarous of methods, terrorization of the civilian population.
On the morning of the 14th May the Dutch Commander-in-Chief of Land and Sea Forces received the threat that, unless resistance were discontinued, Rot-

terdam and Utrecht would be destroyed from the air, and this fate would be shared later by other towns.

Everyone who knows Dutch towns, those rows of houses rising up from the perfectly open polder land, intersected by canals and ditches, where all protection in the form of woods or hills in the environs is lacking, will realize what the execution of this threat on centres of population numbering from 400,000 to 800,000 people would have meant. The fate of Rotterdam, where the threat was carried into effect by an attack of at least fifty bombing aircraft, is an eloquent example of what would have ensued.

Nevertheless, this terrorization would perhaps have been defied if there had been any likelihood whatever that at that moment, or during the following days, support could have been received from our Allies. The latter, however, themselves involved in the intense struggle in Belgium and northern France, were unable to do anything to relieve the Dutch front. Not a single aircraft could be expected to assist in the air defence of Holland; not a single soldier could be landed on the Dutch coast.

In these circumstances the Dutch Supreme Command had only the choice between:

(a) Continuation of the struggle, with the likelihood of being able to maintain the defence for some time longer, but with the certainty that thousands of innocent men, women and children would die a frightful death; or

(b) Agreement to the capitulation of the Dutch forces.

General Winkelman, fully conscious of his responsibility, decided on the latter course (except as regards the troops in Zeeland). In so far as it was placed under the "Commander of the Sea Forces," and therefore not under the Supreme Commander of Land and Sea Forces, the navy was not included in the capitulation. In order to enable as many ships as possible to continue the struggle, on the 14th May all ships were withdrawn from the command of the Commander of the Den Helder position arid allocated to the Commander of the Naval Forces, with orders to proceed to England.

The Commander of the Naval Forces himself left for that country on the 14th May at 1 pm.

In a speech delivered by radio, the Commander-in-Chief explained his decision that same evening to the Dutch population, and in an order of the day of the 15th May thanks were expressed to the troops for what they had done during the campaign (see Appendices III and IV).

On the afternoon of the 14th May the Dutch forces, their hearts filled with despair and rage, laid down their arms.

For every man who had the honour to belong to this force this was the darkest hour of his life.

Chapter Twelve
The Struggle in Zeeland

As far as concerns the defence of Zeeland, the Dutch preparations extended chiefly to the island of Walcheren, with its important harbour of Flushing, and the island of Zuid Beveland.

The seaward defence was in the hands of the Royal Navy, supported by coastal batteries.

With a view to protecting Flushing from the land side, as has already been stated, preparations for defence were made at Bath, along the Zanddijk and the Sloedam. The Haansweert-Wemeldinge Canal was not included in the system of defence except as regards preparing the destruction of the bridges, because owing to the high dykes there and the extensive populated areas it was not quite suited for defence.

The forces entrusted with the defence of Zeeland were weak. Apart from a few battalions of infantry, the occupying forces consisted only of a few batteries of artillery armed with out-of-date material. All that was available for anti-tank defence were a few modern guns, and likewise some 6 cm field guns.

There were some modern anti-aircraft guns at Flushing, but apart from these there was only one battery, armed with out-of-date guns, near the railway bridge at Vlake.

On the remaining Zeeland islands there were merely a few companies of infantry.

During the period preceding the attack, work was hastily carried out to put the preparations for defence on the Bath and in the Zanddijk position into the most effective possible condition. These positions were in fact practically ready, and from the 10th May the flood waters in front of the Bath and the Zanddijk position were raised to the highest possible level.

Except for an air attack on the airfield of Haamstede on the 10th May, there was no enemy action against the Zeeland area.

As early as the 11th May French light troops, which had marched up through Belgium and had been transported by ferry from Zeeland Flanders to Flushing, reached Walcheren. It was agreed with the French commander that the French engineers should cut through the Sloedam.

The harbour installations at Flushing were subjected on that day to German air bombing.

On the 12th May the French continued their march to Zuid Beveland, where they took up their positions behind the Hansweert-Wemeldinge Canal. The canal possessed such attraction for the French as a tank obstacle that, notwithstanding all the other disadvantages attaching to this canal position, they gave it preference above the Zanddijk position lying farther westward.

On the 13th and 14th May the garrison of Zeeland received some reinforcements in the shape of troops who had originally formed part of those occupying the

Meuse and the Raam-Peel position. In this way a new battalion was formed at Serooskerke, which was sent on partly to Noord Beveland and partly to Zeeland Flanders, where new companies were formed in addition from units which had arrived there in their retreat from Brabant via Belgium. The difficulty was that a considerable number of these troops no longer had any arms, because they had had to leave them at the Belgian frontier, owing to a mistake on the part of some local Belgian authorities. The idea of strict neutrality had taken such deep root that even one's own allies were deprived of arms.

The Bath position was abandoned on the 14th May by the troops occupying it, after having been bombed repeatedly from the air, and when it was reported that the enemy had succeeded in reaching the rear of the position by means of a march over the dyke farthest to the south.

It was planned later to reoccupy the position, but this plan could, unfortunately, not be realized, because meanwhile the destruction in the land between the Bath and the Zanddijk position had been carried out, and therefore it had become impossible to use the roads.

The airmen in training at Flushing were meanwhile sent on to northern France.

This personnel was later for the main part attached to the Naval Air Force and made an important contribution towards maintaining the strength of the Dutch bomber squadron, which continued to take part in the European War as part of Coastal Command of the RAF.

On the 15th and 16th May the enemy successively penetrated the positions on the Zanddijk, the Hansweert-Wemeldinge Canal and the Sloe. Lack of artillery, and more especially of anti-aircraft defence, left the Dutch and French troops practically defenceless in the open terrain against the remorseless bombings of the enemy. The town of Middelburg with its magnificent old buildings fell a victim to this merciless mode of warfare.

When the enemy had, by securing possession of the Sloedam, opened up a road for approach to Walcheren, further resistance on this island became impossible, and as many Dutch and French troops as possible were, under continuous air bombing, transported by ferry from Flushing to Zeeland Flanders.

After wandering around through west Belgium to northern France a number of these Dutch units were able to reach England. It was from these troops, strengthened by recruits from all parts of the world, that the Royal Netherlands "Prinses Irene" Brigade was afterwards formed.

All the rest fell into German hands as prisoners, in consequence of the course of events in Belgium and France.

Chapter Thirteen

Final Review

If one looks back at the campaign in Holland, it is a mistake to give paramount consideration to the fact that this campaign, except as regards Zeeland, lasted only five days.

Of course, the time factor is important, and a period of five days is not much in a war that lasts years. But more important is what was achieved during the five days by the troops of the kingdom, and what harvest this period yielded for the general conduct of the war, and for the Allied cause.

It must be put on record with satisfaction, furthermore, that the few troops entrusted with the defence of South Limburg succeeded in carrying out the plan of destruction there completely. The consequence of this was that the advance through South Limburg of the German troops intended for the attack on the Belgian positions on the Albert Canal was delayed. The German tank division, which had to use the bridges over the Albert Canal west of Maastricht, was able to cross the Meuse only on the morning of the 11th May.

The troops on the Meuse-Yssel front between Roermond and Zwolle imposed on the German advance a delay which averaged four to six hours. Of course, these few hours proved very important for the troops in the Valley position farther back and the Raam-Peel position. They were thus enabled quite undisturbed and during daylight to test for the last time the preparations made for defence, and carry out the destructions prepared in the terrain of enemy advance.

The consequence was that the enemy was only able to launch his attack on the Raam-Peel position late on the first day of war, and consequently the troops occupying this position, when the attack proved successful, had the opportunity of withdrawing during the night and continuing resistance on the Zuid Willemsvaart on the second day of war.

The enemy did not even succeed in making contact with tile Valley position on the first day. If it is borne in mind that the Raam-Peel position and the Valley position are only 20 and 40 km respectively from the German frontier, this is certainly no mean result.

The defence of the Raam-Peel position, and the subsequent defence of the Zuid Willemsvaart, together with the work of destruction carried out in Brabant, had the result that the German troops required two and a half days to get into contact with the air-borne infantry landed at Rotterdam and Dordrecht.

The consequence of the delay in North Brabant was that the French mechanized troops of the seventh army were even able to advance to west of Tilburg. If these troops had succeeded in arresting the German advance on the line Turnhout-

Tilburg or Turnhout-Breda, this contact would indeed never have been made, and the campaign in Holland would have taken an entirely different course.

It is stated on the German side that the German Army had calculated that, if the attack on the heart of the country had not had the desired success in the course of the first day, the German troops would have succeeded on the third day of war in making contact with the air-borne troops at Dordrecht and Rotterdam. This calculation, however, was based on the assumption that the Raam-Peel position would be defended by three infantry divisions and one light division. Instead of this, this line, 70 km in length, was held by a single extended division, and not even provided with a single modern gun.

It is to the credit of this division that nevertheless it was able to achieve the same result.

As has already been stated, in view of the impossibility of forming a continuous front with our Belgian Allies, it was a matter of absolute necessity for our Army Command to withdraw the Third Army Corps and the Light Division from North Brabant, in order to cover the south front. How the fighting in Brabant would have gone if these troops had remained there remains an open question. Judging, however, by what happened some days later in Belgium and northern France, it would have had no influence on the final result.

The fact that: the Third Army Corps and the Light Division were not withdrawn before the first day of war is not entirely justifiable from the strategic point of view, but was a matter of political necessity.

It is a source of great satisfaction to observe that, the German attack on the heart of the country, the object of which was to break down the resistance on the very first day of war and to seize the centre of government, failed completely owing to the heroic struggle of the First Army Corps and the young depot troops.

It is very regrettable, however, that the First Army Corps was in this way diverted from its principal task, and was likewise unable to expel the enemy from the island of Ysselmonde and the island of Dordrecht by a concentrated attack in conjunction with the Light Division. It must, however, not be forgotten in this connection that the military position in the heart of the country remained a difficult one till the last moment. Not only was there a continuously active fifth column, but, owing to the complete supremacy of the German air force, there might at any moment have been a repetition of what had happened in the first days of the war – namely, an attack by air-borne troops on the heart of the country. Owing to this, considerable numbers of the First Army Corps were tied down there, though these forces were so badly needed for the struggle on the southern front of the Holland Fortress and the Valley position.

The defence of the Valley position lasted from the morning of the second day of war to the evening of the fourth. The absence of reserves was the reason why the position had to be abandoned after a local break-through. It is simply a matter of impossibility to carry on a defence without reserves. Notwithstanding this, the defence of the Grebbeberg will remain a proud memory in the history of the Dutch Army.

FINAL REVIEW 67

The fight for the fortifications at the Kornwerderzand was successful to the last moment, and once again, too, it was seen that Dutch troops provided with modern material need fear no antagonist.

Finally, the defence of Zeeland was a less successful episode. Here, however, it must not be forgotten that it is not feasible for a small number of troops crowded together in narrow defiles in open country, without artillery support and practically without air cover, to maintain itself against a modern opponent who has complete command of the air.

The Dutch forces, owing to the relative strength of the armies, were compelled from the outset to limit themselves to defence. Though it may be true that as a form of warfare defence is stronger than attack, it is no less true that the initiative lies with the attacker, and that the will of the defender is from the outset subordinated to that of the attacker.

Thus the attacker has the advantage of the choice of the place and the time of the operation, and can take care to be the stronger at the decisive fighting points which he selects. Consequently the attacker, notwithstanding the fact that the total force employed by him was less than the total strength of the Dutch forces, was by far the stronger at the points where the decision was sought: the southern part of the Valley position, North Brabant, and the south front of the Holland Fortress. The defender must keep troops in readiness everywhere, because parts of the front where nothing happens today may tomorrow be the scenes of powerful attacks. It is inevitable therefore especially when the campaign is of such short duration as was the case in Holland, that large numbers of defending troops do not even come into action. This is what happened in the case of the troops of the Fourth and Third Army Corps and the battalions in the delaying lines, whose sectors lay outside the German axes of march.

That is the drawback inherent in every defence.

Nevertheless – and let this be the harvest which the Dutch defence yielded for our Allies – the struggle in Holland produced the result that for five days, plus the time required for regrouping and transfer to the fighting areas in Belgium and northern France – another four days at least – a German force of not less than 250,000 men remained fully engaged, and this force sustained heavy losses, particularly as regards its aircraft.

If we bear in mind that between the 10th and the 19th May the following events took place in Belgium:

(a) the battle for the Albert Canal,

(b) the battles for the Dyle position,

(c) the battle on the Sedan-Namur-Meuse front,

(d) the retreat from the Dyle to the Scheldt -

the Dutch resistance really made a substantial contribution to the relief of our Allies fighting farther to the south.

More important than these positive facts, however, is the spirit which was displayed in the defence. A nation which, even after a long period of peace, is ready and willing to make every sacrifice called for to maintain its independence cannot perish.

The Dutch forces gave all that was in their power to give.

Let us hope that in future the fighting forces of the Netherlands will be supplied with all the material means they may require, so that their splendid fighting qualities will not be wasted.

List of Abbreviations used in the Appendices and Maps

Note. – The term Regiment in Dutch is equivalent to Brigade in English except in the case of mounted units, including those which have since been mechanized.

In the text the English equivalent has been used throughout. In the maps and appendices, however, initials referring to the Dutch military terminology have had to be retained.

AA	Anti-aircraft guns
AC	Army Corps
ACT	Army Corps Train
AR	Artillery Regiment
C	Commander
CCLSF	Commander-in-Chief Land and Sea Forces
CMA	Corps of Horse Artillery
CP	Company of Pioneers
Com AAMG	Company of Anti-aircraft Machine Gunners
CR	Cyclists Regiment
Ch R	Chasseurs Regiment
DC	Divisional Commander
Div	Division
Div Tr	Divisional Train
FB	Frontier Battalion
Gr R	Grenadier Regiment
HQ	Headquarters
HR	Hussars Regiment
IR	Infantry Regiment
L	Long (applied to guns)
Lt Div	Light Division
MHR	Motor Cyclist Hussars Regiment
MMG (C)	Medium Machine Gun Company
MMG (Sq)	Medium Machine Gun Squadron
Mot Bat	Battalion of Motor Trains
Mot Com	Company of Motor Trains
Mot Reg	Motor Train Regiment
Signals	Signals Unit
St HQ	Staff Headquarters

Army Corps, Divisions, Battalions of Infantry, Brigades of Artillery and Army Corps Troops are denoted by Roman figures, Regiments by Arabic figures.

Appendix I

Distribution of the Principal Dutch Forces over the Various Theatres of Operation

A – Troops intended for Subsidiary Strategic Duties.

Troops intended for delaying action in the land east of the Yssel:
5 FB
9 FB
16 FB
19 FB
22 FB

Troops intended for territorial defence in the northern provinces:
1 FB
12 FB
33 IR (min I)
36 IR

Troops intended for delay in the southern part of North Brabant (later posted to the southern front of Holland Fortress):
FB – Ch R.
3 – FB
6 – FB

Troops for delaying action in the Raam-Peel position:
I – 3 IR
I – 6 IR
III – 14 IR
II – 2 IR
I – 13 IR
II – 17 IR
4 FB
27 IR
30 IR
II – 41 IR
20 AR (8cm st)

Troops for territorial defence of south Limburg:
13 FB
37 IR

APPENDIX I

Troops for delaying action on river line Meuse-Meuse-Waal Canal-Yssel:
2 FB
8 FB
11 FB
15 FB
17 FB
26 IR
35 IR
41 IR (min II)
43 IR

Troops for territorial defence of Zeeland:
14 FB
28 IR
17 AR (8 cm steel)
Coast Artillery

B – Troops intended as Security Forces on the Fronts of the Holland Fortress, for Occupation of the Den Helder Position and of Important Objectives in the Interior. *

FB – Gr R
7 FB
10 FB
18 FB
20 FB
21 FB
23 IR
25 IR
28 IR
31 IR
32 IR
I/33 IR
34 IR
39 IR
40 IR
42 IR
45 IR
1 MHR
14 AR (L 12)
22 AR (15 L 24)
23 AR (7 field)
Coastal Artillery

* Six battalions of these troops were embodied in the strength of the III AC in order to replace the units left behind in the Raam-Peel position.

72 MILITARY OPERATIONS OF THE DUTCH ARMY

C. Troops intended for the Principal Struggle.

THE FIELD ARMY
(a) Troops in Valley Position

II AC (Staff; Signals)
   II Div (Staff; Signals)
      10 IR
      15 IR
      22 IR
      2 MMG
      4 AR
      2 CP
   IV Div (Staff; Signals)
      8 IR
      19 IR
      11 IR
      4 MMG
      8 AR
      4 CP
   Corps Troops
      12 AR
      II ACT
      2 Supply, etc., Tr 4 HR
      II Mot Bat
      Brigade AA guns
      3, 7, Com AAMG

IV AC (Staff; Signals)
   VII Div (Staff; Signals)
      7 IR
      18 IR
      20 IR
      7 MMG
      1 AR
      7 CP
   VIII Div (Staff; Signals)
      5 IR
      16 IR
      21 IR
      8 MMG
      5 AR
      8 CP
   Corps Troops
      9 AR
      IV ACT
      4 Supply, etc., Tr 1, 5 HR
      IV Mot Bat

Brigade AA guns
4, 8, Com AAMG

(b) Defence of Area between Meuse and Lek

Independent Brigade Group A
   Staff
   Signals
   44 IR
   46 IR
   16 AR (8 cm st)
Independent Brigade Group B
   Staff
   Signals
   24 IR
   29 IR*
   21 AR (8 cm st)

* Of this regiment, two battalions were stationed on the Brabant shore of the Meuse between Grave and Appeltern.

6 Com AAMG
Army Troops in Valley Position
   AR 13 (12 L)
   15 (15 L 15)
   18 (12 L)
   19 (12 L)
   Mot Reg

(c) Defence of the Waal to South Front of Holland Fortress

III AC (Staff; Signals)
   V Div (Staff; Signals)
      2 IR (min II)
      13 IR (min I)
      17 IR (min II)
      5 MMG
      3 AR
      5 CP
   VI Div (Staff; Signals)
      3 IR (min I)
      6 IR (min I)
      14 IR (min III)
      6 MMG
      7 AR
      6 CP
   Lt Div (Staff; Signals)
      1 CR
      2 CR
      2 MHR
      MMG (Sq)

CMA
Div Tr
5 Supply, etc Tr Mot Com
Corps Troops
 11 AR
 III ACT
 3 Supply, etc., Tr 2 HR
 III Mot Bat
 Brigade AA Guns
 5, 9 Com AAMG

    (d) General Reserve (under Orders of CC LSF)
I AC (Staff; Signals)
 I Div (Staff; Signals)
  Cr R
  Ch R
  4 IR
  1 MMG
  2 AR
  1 CP
 III Div (Staff; Signals)
  1 IR
  9 IR
  12 IR
  3 MMG
  6 AR
  3 CP
 Corps Troops
  10 AR
  1 ACT
  1 Supply, etc., Tr 3 HR
  1 Mot Bat
  Bridgade AA Guns
  1, 2 Com AAMG

Appendix II

This is an English translation of a German order captured near The Hague in the course of operations.

Operation Orders

II Bn. Inf Regt 65
In the Field
16th April, 1940.

1. Information with regard to the enemy will be issued under separate cover.

2. XXII Inf Div with 1 Bn 2 Parachute Rifle Regt under command will surround and occupy The Hague, the capital of Holland. The division will land from the air on ....* [* Note by the General Staff – The date was not given in the order. It was however, 10th May 1940] on the following landing grounds:
   Landing Ground No 1 (about 10 km north of The Hague) – reinforced Inf Regt 47.
   Landing Ground No. 2 (sports field about 2 km south of The Hague) – reinforced II Bn Inf Regt 65.
   Landing Ground No. 3 (about 2 km southeast of The Hague) – reinforced Inf Regt 65 (less 2 Bn).
The Air Force will attack enemy aerodromes, landing grounds and installations and will cover the landing of the division.

3. II Bn Inf Regt 65 (less 6 and 8 Coys) supported by 13 Coy (infantry guns) of the regiment and 1 Pl 6 Coy 2 Parachute Rifle Regt will occupy and hold the landing ground so that landing can be continued thereon until M+ 1 day. It will also block all roads leading from The Hague towards the southwest and will stop all traffic in both directions. The battalion will also carry out continuous reconnaissance towards the line Monster-Poeldijk and the south-western edge of The Hague.
   1 Pl 6 Coy 2 Parachute Rifle Regt (Lieut Gungelmann) will jump 32 minutes before the battalion is landed, seize the landing ground and expel the enemy from the sand dunes around Kijkduin.

4. To perform this task units will carry out the following orders:

   (a) One Pl 5 Coy immediately after landing will occupy Loosduinen and will stop all traffic in both directions on:
   - Roads leading southeast from Poeldijk and Wateringen (1).
   - North-eastern exits from The Hague (Hout-Weg) (2).
   - Loosduinsche street (3). (See attached sketch.)

   An elevated observation post will be located and occupied (a church tower, if possible).

   Continuous reconnaissance will be carried out as far as Poeldijk, Wateringen and the south-eastern edge of The Hague.

At the latter point contact will be established with Inf Regt 65.

(b) One Pl 5 Coy will block the south-eastern exits of The Hague at Van Meerdervoort-Laan (4) and Sport-Laan (5) and stop the traffic in both directions. It will also occupy and hold Kijkduin (6), paying particular attention to the sea front.

An elevated observation post will be established.

Continuous reconnaissance (two patrols) will be carried out through the sand dunes in a northerly direction, as far as the south-western edge of Scheveningen and in a south-westerly direction as far as Terheiden.

(c) One Pl 5 Coy will remain at my disposal. Its initial task will be the AA defence of the landing ground. Subsequent tasks will probably be:

(i) Requisitioning of transport and bicycles for 5 and 7 Coys.

(ii) Erection of a P/W cage.

(iii) Erection of a salvage dump.

(iv) Attack towards the harbour of Scheveningen.

Continuous reconnaissance (a bicycle patrol) will be maintained along the road Loosduinen-Terheiden-Monster as far as those villages.

(d) HQ 5 Coy Inf Regt 65 will be in Loosduinen at road junction towards Poeldijk.

(e) 1 Pl 6 Coy 2 Parachute Rifle Regt will withdraw detachments holding the landing ground on relief by 5 Coy Inf Regt 65, and will then reinforce and widen road blocks on the road Loosduinen-Monster towards the southwest.

(f) HQ II Bn Inf Regt 65 will be established in the Van Meerdervoort-Laan (probably some 300 metres northeast of landing ground No. 2). It will also establish an observation post with a scissors telescope. W/T communication will be established with Div HQ and 5 Coy.

(g) The MO will establish a RAP.

(h) 7 and 13 (infantry gun) Coys will arrive by air four and seven hours respectively after the initial landing. They will be given their tasks on arrival at Landing Ground No 2.

5. The boundary between the battalion and the remainder of reinforced Inf Regt 65 for holding the landing ground, reconnaissance and encirclement of The Hague will be as follows:

Naaldwi J K (incl Inf Regt 65) – Uithofspolder (incl II Bn Inf Regt 65) centre of the southern edge of The Hague.

APPENDIX II 77

6. A civilian representative will be attached to every commander and second-in-command in the battalion, who will be kept informed as to the situation and the task of the battalion.

Lieut Lingner, 5 Coy Inf Regt 65, is detailed as representative of the battalion commander until the latter arrives.

7. Constant watchfulness against air and ground attacks will be maintained at all times. Captured enemy weapons will be utilized for AA defence. Troops will remain dispersed. The landing ground will be kept free of personnel.

8. Trenches with splinter-proof covering will be constructed immediately for outposts and reserves for protection against aerial bombardment.

9. For blocking roads, any material which can be found should be used, including carts, motor-cars and trams. Drawbridges will be raised.

10. Short situation reports will be rendered at frequent intervals.

(Signed) Major, OC Battalion.
Distribution: OC II Bn
5 Coy
7 Coy
13 Coy
6 Coy 2 Parachute Rifle Regt.

Appendix III

Speech delivered by radio by the Commander-in-Chief of the Land and Sea Forces to the people of Holland on the evening of the 14th May

We have had to lay down our arms because no other course was open to us. We were all firmly resolved to defend our country to the utmost. I, however, who in my capacity as Commander-in-Chief of the Land and Sea Forces received all reports, knew with complete certainty that this utmost had today been reached. Our soldiers have fought with a courage which will never be forgotten. The contest, however, was too unequal. Our troops had to face technical methods and contrivances against which the highest human courage is of no avail. They fell in their thousands for the freedom of Holland.

The air forces which we still have at our disposal are so small that they are practically unable any longer to support our troops in ground operations. Against the German air supremacy, moreover, our other means of defence, such as our anti-aircraft guns, had only a limited effect, notwithstanding the bravery and skill with which the AA batteries performed their task. Thus our troops were exposed to destructive bombing by German aircraft.

And not they alone. Among the civil population, the women and children, the air war claimed innumerable victims. In our densely populated country, with its many towns, it is difficult in bombing from the air to distinguish between military and non-military objectives. Rotterdam, which was this afternoon bombed by the German air force, has suffered the wretched fate of total war. Utrecht and other great centres of population would have to share the fate of Rotterdam within a very short time.

Left almost entirely to ourselves for our defence, we were not in a position to safeguard our country and our civil population against his violence. It was hard facts which compelled me to come to my very grave decision; we have discontinued the struggle.

I quite realize that this decision will come as a shock to many of our people. Let them understand, however, that at this moment I represent the Netherlands Government in this country, and that therefore I was not only entitled, but also bound to decide in the manner required by the interests of the Dutch people in these circumstances.

It is to me absolutely undeniable that this interest necessitates the discontinuance of the utterly unequal struggle, in order that the latter may not claim still more innocent victims. All who are able to grasp the full extent of my responsibility will understand how hard it must be for me to come to this decision. Yet it could not be otherwise.

Appendix IV

Order of the day of the Dutch Commander-in-Chief of Land and Sea Forces on the 15th May

I find myself impelled once more to give expression to the very great gratitude and admiration which I feel for the devotion, faithfulness and bravery which have been evidenced by all the forces of the Royal Netherlands Army and the Royal Navy in the struggle which we finally had to abandon in view of the overpowering weapons of our opponent.

I have in mind first and foremost the many members of the Dutch forces who have laid down their lives in performance of their duty to Queen and country.

Officers, non-commissioned officers and men of the Netherlands Forces, you have proved that you were prepared to make the last sacrifice for the righteous cause of your country. I know that you would have been ready to continue the struggle if I had demanded this. I did not demand it, however, because I did not wish to expose my troops any longer, without defence, to destructive bombings and machine gunning from the air, and because I desired to safeguard our towns against destruction.

The sacrifices made by our people have certainly not been in vain, for Holland has shown the world that she is willing to sacrifice her wealth and her blood for the high ideal of her independence.

Related titles published by Helion & Company

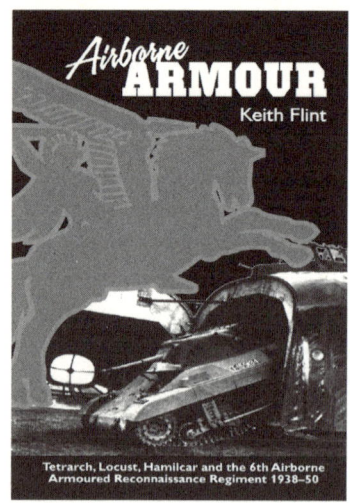

Airborne Armour: Tetrarch, Locust, Hamilcar and the 6th Airborne Armoured Reconnaissance Regiment 1938–50
Keith Flint
224pp   Hardback
ISBN 1 874622 37 X

For Rex & For Belgium: Léon Degrelle and Walloon Political & Military Collaboration 1940–45
Eddy de Bruyne and Marc Rikmenspoel
304pp   Hardback
ISBN 1 874622 32 9

A selection of forthcoming titles

The Royal Corps of Signals: Unit Histories of the Corps (1920–2001) and Its Antecedents
(paperback reprint)
Cliff Lord and Graham Watson   ISBN 1 874622 92 2

The Black Devil's March – A Doomed Odyssey: The 1st Polish Armoured Division 1939–45
Evan McGilvray   ISBN 1 874622 42 6

SOME ADDITIONAL SERVICES FROM HELION & COMPANY

BOOKSELLERS
- over 20,000 military books available
- four 100-page catalogues issued every year
- unrivalled stock of foreign language material, particularly German

BOOKSEARCH
- free professional booksearch service; no search fees, no obligation to buy

Want to find out more? Our website is the best place to learn more about Helion & Co. It features online book catalogues, special offers, complete information about our own books (including features on in-print and forthcoming titles, sample extracts and reviews), a shopping cart system and a secure server for credit card transactions, plus much more besides!

HELION & COMPANY
26 Willow Road, Solihull, West Midlands, B91 1UE, England
Tel 0121 705 3393   Fax 0121 711 4075
Website: http://www.helion.co.uk